"Leading from the Edge of the Inside *lays out a convincing argument that business requires a new operating system. The essential conversations are a framework for dramatically increasing value creation for customers, employees, and owners. I could almost hear these conversations taking place in environments in which I have been engaged with management teams. This approach will yield much better outcomes!"*

Carole Whittaker, Ph.D.

founding and emeritus member of the Board of the Arizona Enneagram Association

Enneagram teacher and spiritual director

"Leading from the Edge of the Inside *is a leadership story about the journey into deep awareness. The essential conversations and their foundational practices represent a profound breakthrough. By discovering the invisible patterns that block your management team your ability to differentiate your company will dramatically improve."*

Tim Call

SVP Vistage International

LEADING FROM THE EDGE OF THE INSIDE

Embracing the Heart of
Business Leadership

JIM MOATS

Jim Moats – jim@peer-place.com

Some names and identifying details have been changed to protect the privacy of individuals. The author has tried to recreate events, locales, and conversations from memories of them. In order to maintain their anonymity, in some instances names of individuals and places, some identifying characteristics and details such as physical properties, occupations, and places of residence were changed.

Poem by Judy Brown, A Leader's Guide to Reflective Practice. judysorumbrown.com

Editing by Cara Highsmith, Highsmith Creative Services,
www.highsmithcreative.com

Cover and Interior Design by Mitchell Shea

ISBN 978-1-7339502-0-6
ISBN 978-1-7339502-1-3
Library of Congress Control Number:2019907938

Printed in the United States of America

First Edition 14 13 12 11 10 / 10 9 8 7 6 5 4 3 2 1

NEWTYPE
PUBLISHING

To my son Nick - one of the most courageous people I know.

Acknowledgements

This book emerged through my work with management teams and Vistage members in Seattle, Washington. I wish to thank Curt Altig for offering me an initial framework to test my early ideas. Without his encouragement this book would never have been written. I also wish to thank the many CEO and executive members of the Vistage groups I have chaired and the management teams I have worked with. My interactions with them around the ideas I was trying to articulate in our groups over many years, shaped each of the pages in this book. I also want to thank my colleagues, the Vistage Chairs who have encouraged me throughout this endeavor.

I want to thank writing coach Rob Jolles for pushing me in the very early stages of this manuscript and my editor Cara Highsmith for the depth of commitment displayed throughout the entire creative process. A special thank you to Jim Henderson for generously advising me and also for connecting me to expert help.

Also, this book has been shaped by several very brave people who serve as my alpha and beta readers: Leslie Osborne, Tom Zahniser, Tom Paladino, Carole Whitaker, Tim Call, and John Nichols. The endless hours they invested to help me bring order out of chaos exceeded my expectations. I want to acknowledge my friend Michael Stuart. Our weekly conversations strengthened my spirit.

I am especially happy to be able to acknowledge and thank my wife, Becky, for her continuing role in my spiritual development, especially for the way she models a life of prayer. Our morning conversations are among my life's most fulfilling experiences.

Thanks be to God!

CONTENTS

LEADING FROM THE EDGE OF THE INSIDE

INTRODUCTION

The primary concern that occupies the minds of most company leaders is solving problems, and it becomes the focus of most management team meetings. I want to help you and your management team tackle problem solving from a new perspective, using an approach I developed during my own leadership journey.

While I was the majority owner of a software company, I became a member of Vistage International—the largest CEO membership organization in the world. A Vistage CEO group consists of up to sixteen CEOs of privately owned companies. After I sold the software company, I decided to become a Vistage chair. That role became a learning lab for me to study patterns of thinking, feeling, and behaving that consistently sabotage the best intentions of CEOs.

This is how it all started. Susan, the regional president for a public company and a very bright, take-charge kind of leader, set the tone for something special to happen within her company: she demonstrated a willingness to be vulnerable in front of her employees, something few leaders do voluntarily.

In our initial meeting, when she asked me if I could help her create a high-performance leadership team, I asked what success would look like for her. She answered that there was an impasse around growth that originated within her management team, but she couldn't articulate exactly what success would look like.

In the next weeks, as we met more frequently, it became clear she was determined to change the way she led her team, so I asked if she would let me experiment. She agreed, though she was unsure of what I had in mind.

I suggested we convene monthly meetings with her management team and conduct periodic 360° reviews for each person.[1] We decided she would be the first to have her boss, peers, and subordinates review her based on sixty leadership behaviors, and these would be compared to how she views herself. Next, we would identify the changes she wanted to make based on their feedback—what I call the leading edge of her development—and she would share her results at an all-company gathering while asking them to hold her accountable.

Eighteen months later, Susan came to me and said, "Profits and revenue are up dramatically, and I need to know specifically what caused this." When I told her I wasn't sure, she asked me to find out.

After scratching my head, it occurred to me I could probably find student interns at the University of Washington to help me evaluate what was happening. I felt unprepared when I called Dr. Terry Mitchell at the Foster School of Business because I knew he would want details that I didn't have. But this was my Hail Mary pass.

In our conversation, I described what I'd been up to and asked for help. He asked, "What's unique about your work?"

I said, "Not much, other than you can only enter this program through the door of humility."

He paused, then said, "Say that again."

He told me the university had a team researching how humility in leadership impacted business results. They, too, had noticed how traditional leadership models focused on problem-solving was producing diminishing returns.

That's when I met Brad. Brad was completing his PhD work through the University of Washington on this topic but lacked a practical place to conduct his research. Synchronicity was at work.

Brad assembled his research team and Susan agreed to let him complete a study on her company. His team analyzed financials, accumulated 360° review data, completed interviews, and then triangulated the data to form conclusions.

In a nutshell, their findings indicated that the practices and rituals sustained through recurring monthly meetings resulted in an unusually high level of mutual trust. Further, because of this trust, organic collaboration emerged throughout the region and this was responsible for the increased revenue and profit growth. It seemed that employee engagement had risen beyond our wildest hopes. As leadership awareness grew–performance did as well.

This is how the seeds for this book took root in my heart. I now see that the initial practices this team employed around management team interactions, which I will describe later, strengthened each person's *inner capacity* to collaborate. As awareness of self, others, and shared awareness of each other became more accessible, their capacity to transcend tension grew. Awareness monitors the inward and outward signals that indicate how well you are doing and helps you intervene in the patterns that have historically sidetracked your management team. We started by digging into self-awareness.

My Journey to Self-Awareness

I realize now that my own journey of inner awareness prepared the way for my work with Susan and, ultimately, this book.

Year after year, the CEO members of my Vistage group expressed an interest in learning more about strategic planning, but by the end of the second quarter, their execution often no longer mapped to the strategy they had laid out. Despite their best "thinking," their companies had become sidetracked.

Why? Many said it was the accelerating rate of change in the external world that was solely responsible, but I disagreed. I realize this is a bold statement, so I'll back it up with another:

While I've never seen a business problem that couldn't be solved, I have seen business leaders who struggle with being fully present to reality.

While I've never seen a *business problem* that couldn't be solved, I have seen *business leaders* who struggle with being fully present to reality.

Business isn't rocket science—the mechanics are straightforward. What isn't straightforward is the inner landscape of a leader. Reactionary patterns of behavior—and the thinking and feeling beneath them—are sidetracking CEOs and business leaders, and having in-depth, important conversations about their businesses with them has become increasingly difficult.

In 1968, I was assigned to the Combined Intelligence Center in Vietnam. As an order of battle specialist/intelligence analyst, I sifted through volumes of intelligence data to identify the patterns of enemy units. I learned to take facts and project them into possibilities. I learned to remove the mystery and help create battle plans. I became an advocate for sound thinking, hard-nosed strategy, and strong-willed execution, and these skills served me well in my roles in the corporate environment. As far as I was concerned, soft skills, and those who had them, were simply taking up seats on the bus.

After leadership roles in three Fortune 500 companies, I left the corporate world to lead a small, underfunded, international not-for-profit operating in Central Asia. I told myself I was giving back, but in reality, I was trying to fill an inner void. Something was missing.

As I moved into my second year, the quality of my sleep deteriorated and my energy dropped. I found myself putting off important phone calls and meetings. This was unlike anything I had experienced, and I tried to fake it for too long.

Eventually, in a conversation with my VP, I admitted the obvious: I was losing my edge. Kathy was a seasoned international pro, having lived and grown up in the international diplomatic scene, and she understood people.

She helped me put into words what I had been feeling, and then she said, "I want you to do two things: contact Ray Vath, a psychiatrist, and make an appointment with Lorraine Picker, a Christian therapist." By the end of the week, I had done both.

Ray Vath diagnosed me as clinically depressed. At this point, I was so tired that about all I could do was sit around, so it was helpful to know the cause. More important, Ray helped me understand that I had been walking down a very dark road by attaching my self-worth to being successful. This began to open a window into self-awareness.

But, it was my work with Lorraine that helped me in a way I never could have anticipated.

Lorraine seemed battle savvy and carried a calm awareness. Her words were just enough to guide me into a deeper place beyond my discomfort. I felt strangely secure with her.

In our sessions, Lorraine asked a few straightforward questions that I tried to answer as best I could. Then, she asked me if she could pray. While I was in no way prepared for this, something told me this was okay.

One afternoon during the time I was working with Lorraine, my oldest son, Brian, didn't come home from school. After making numerous calls to track him down, my wife was told to call the school counselor.

The counselor explained that she and Brian had talked, and she requested that my wife and I come to school the next day to meet with the two of them. I was shocked. *How dare she become involved like this with my family?*

At the meeting, she explained that Brian was not in trouble, but the situation at home had come to a head—it needed to be addressed. In many emotional words, Brian explained that I was controlling and that he didn't want to be around me. While this was very difficult to hear, what made it even more excruciating was to see my wife nodding her head in agreement. I was being invited to delve further into self-awareness.

I had started to reconnect to my essence—my true inner self that wasn't guided by the need to be successful—and I noticed a point of choice that was becoming more available to me.

My work with Lorraine had created space within me where I could begin to see and accept parts of myself that I did not want to perpetuate. I had started to reconnect to my essence—my true inner self that wasn't guided by the need to be successful—and I noticed a *point of choice* that was becoming more available to me. The choice was to pause, breathe, and let truth guide me by unhooking from my thoughts. That day with Brian, a deeper presence invited me to let go, and, fortunately, I said yes. That was the day the sap started running again!

THE DEEP WORK

Science is now discovering what Carl Jung coined "the collective unconscious," Saint Paul labeled "the mind of Christ," and the Sufis call "the general mind." Scientists now describe this idea as consciousness.

Wisdom traditions associated with major religions have understood this concept for hundreds and even thousands of years, but now science is accelerating its grasp of it, calling this relatively young field contemplative neuroscience. Neuroscience and psychology now explain what I was going though as the experience of integration; religion would call it an awakening.

James Newton (a gifted consultant hired by Vistage) believed that to help CEOs "become more effective," they needed the capacity to ask themselves questions that prompted a deeper dive into their reactive emotional and behavioral patterns. None of us were very well equipped to do this; yet, because of my work with Lorraine, the idea wasn't entirely foreign to me, and I was enthusiastic about developing new skills to facilitate inner work. This journey has been about my own transformation as much as it has been about helping others.

As my work with Susan and the University of Washington wrapped up, I found myself teaching a class about how to maximize leadership and the spiritual life.

Part of the course work included books by Richard Foster, such as *Celebration of Discipline* and *Freedom of Simplicity*. As I read his work, I could tell his view was wider than many. He seemed both practical and mystical. He expected the spiritual journey to transform life, especially habituated reactive patterns. I was attracted to this.

I tried to learn about the influences that had impacted Foster's life. I discovered that one of the people who had greatly impacted him was John Main.

John Main (1926-1982) was a Benedictine monk who taught Christian meditation and began meditation groups that met at Ealing Abbey, his monastery in West London, England, and, later, in Montreal, Canada. Born in London of an Irish family,

Main found himself, in the last year of World War II, employed as a radiographer in an intelligence unit. His job was to pinpoint the exact location of enemy radio signals while working behind enemy lines and forward them to headquarters.[2] This experience of receiving and transmitting signals played a powerful role in his spiritual formation and, ultimately, mine.

John Main believed that—like radio signals—meditation helps us tune in to the Spirit. After reading Main's books, I started meditating twice daily. Although I didn't understand it at the time, thirteen years later, I see that mediation softened my reactive mind by removing clutter and allowed me to become more aware of my connection to Spirit.

After a few months of following this daily practice, my wife came to me and said, "I don't understand what this is or why you are doing it; but, whatever it is, keep it up. You are different." She went on to say that I was more patient, that I listened better, and I wasn't in such a hurry. I hadn't realized my behavior had changed, but others noticed.

As I continued my practice, I found that my capacity to be present with reality was expanding. My listening grew and my ability to better understand the dysfunction I saw sidetracking management team conversations became clear.

By this point I began to understand how my personal experience with depression, inner healing, my son Brian, and meditation, had combined with my business experience to birth a way of seeing and perceiving that had previously been unavailable. Helping CEOs and management teams shift their thinking, feeling, and behaving became a calling. Company leadership, especially in privately owned companies, needed to become much more sustainable and my hunger to learn grew exponentially.

Toward Sustainability

Nearly all owners I've worked with express a latent desire around the midlife point in their ownership role to continue finding meaning as an owner while carrying less financial burden and becoming less involved in the day-to-day without worry. This book is written to help owners, executives, and their guides achieve this goal by creating sustainable companies.

In the early stages of your ownership journey, your company and your leadership team operated from within a certain frame of reference. If your expertise was sales, engineering, finance, operations, or administration, your frame of reference was initially defined by that mindset. As impasses accumulated, the limits of your frame of reference became obvious, and like most of us, your search for a new framework began. Perhaps you read books or found a helpful guide. Now, shift to today and ask yourself, "Will my management team achieve sustainability so that I have more freedom?"

A frame of reference is what we know about a mindset. Each frame of reference, and the people who operate within it, have commonly held patterns of thinking, feeling, and behaving. These frames of reference become deeply grooved by experience and the fields of emotion that flow through them. Frames of reference help us navigate the unknown. They are like scaffolding. They help our understanding grow and yet they each have limitations.

When we see the limitations of frame of reference, we instantly find ourselves beyond it. We usually arrive at this place when we experience leadership impasses that a particular mindset (frame of reference) can't navigate. For each person who understands the old frame of reference, they are able to see it in a totally new light, and in some cases, it is seen as no longer applicable; those who do not yet see still work within the old frame of reference. While we can all see obsolete frames of reference in politics, religion, and economics, shifting our frame of reference (mindset), while still operating within it, is nearly impossible. Business challenges give us the opportunity to shift more quickly through organic collaboration.

WHERE THE SHIFT OCCURS

Many leaders occupy the same frames of reference for most of their careers. Using the idea of a spiral of growth and the nine conversations we describe in the following chapters, you and your management team will be led through ever-expanding frames of reference.

Throughout these chapters, I raise the idea of a management team deliberately working to create a sustainable company and address how that can be achieved.

Becoming sustainable means that value creation has become institutionalized and that a management team no longer depends on one person or owner for direction or energy. It also means that value creation continues to evolve and deepen so the long-term needs of your staff are being met at greater and greater levels. I have identified four levels of sustainability, which will be outlined in greater detail later, that encapsulate the conversations we move through. Level I includes Value Creation, Execution, and Growth. Level II holds Leader Effectiveness and Management Team Coherence. Level III is Collaboration and Connection. And Level IV involves Inner Fluency.

These pages tell the story of why the nine conversations are important and how to use them in your management team meetings. To address the journey toward sustainability, you have to challenge your current frames of reference. Challenging long-held views or frames of reference initially creates confusion, frustration, and curiosity. Throughout the chapters, I'll be asking you to take a close look at yourself and your management team by climbing onto your personal viewing platform through a series of questions. These questions will help deepen what you are learning. I promise that if you do this work, you will find a more fulfilling way forward.

Through this book, I hope to change the way you think about the concept we call a "company" and the way you and your management team work together as leaders. By doing this, I believe you will come to enjoy the work you do because it has become much more meaningful and sustainable.

CHAPTER 1
LEADING FROM THE EDGE OF THE INSIDE

After spending much of the first twenty years of my business life in Fortune 500 leadership roles, I arrogantly thought I knew what caused organic growth to occur. During my time at American Express, I completed three acquisitions in the technology space, all of which were eventually resold to other companies. Two years after my departure, a top-tier New York consulting company asked if they could meet with me to talk through my perspective on why that happened. I said yes, on one condition: that I receive a complete, unabridged copy of their finished report.

While I hadn't understood what had happened in those last years with American Express, I did have a sense of what might have taken place and the report helped me piece this together: I had felt an increasing void around the work I was doing. Even today, thirty years later, it's hard to explain that feeling, but I now understand it as being related to a lack of purpose.

When I was part of a cohesive team that was making a difference in the world, work felt like play. I felt as though my life mattered and I belonged. My work had meaning that invited my best effort. Over the last three years of my time there, that had disintegrated. I can see now that we had prioritized money, share price, and personal gain. The company had simply become a strategy for getting rich. With its purpose fulfilled and nothing important to replace it, we lost our way, and ultimately this company's capacity to create value deteriorated. Unfortunately, thousands of employees paid the price.

I learned that companies can become someone's personal strategy. For the owner, CEO, executives, and every employee, this construct we call a "company" is a tool in the service of fulfilling a "felt need." But almost no companies or CEOs conduct the deeper exploration of how those needs can be brought to the surface and upgraded in the service of sustainability. We simply don't know how to talk about these kinds of bedrock issues. I'm not talking about values work, which is very common. Values sit on top of felt needs, and unless these are honored and upgraded, values do not shift even when we try to manage behavior. Without identifying a noble purpose for our work, meaning becomes fragmented and sustainability is nearly impossible.

Values sit on top of felt needs, and unless these are honored and upgraded, values do not shift even when we try to manage behavior.

Creating and maintaining a sustainable company requires engagement. Jim Clifton, the CEO of Gallup, in his introduction to their 2016 State of the American Workforce study, says:

> The American workforce has more than 100 million full-time employees. One-third of those employees are what Gallup calls engaged at work. They love their jobs and make their organization and America better every day. At the other end, 16% of employees are actively disengaged—they are miserable in the workplace and destroy what the most engaged employees build. The remaining 51% of employees are not engaged—they're just there.[3] These figures indicate an American leadership philosophy that simply doesn't work anymore.

What Goes on Inside?

When Ted, the CEO of a healthcare company, asked me to help him with his management team, I was excited. They were bright and confident, and I knew they would challenge me.

As I oriented them to our process, which will be detailed through this book, the looks on their faces told me that they couldn't begin to imagine how this experience would help them become more effective. At critical times like this, I venture off the traditional road map and engage with people directly, so I asked, "What goes on inside of you?"

You can imagine the silence that accompanied their stares. This was clearly a subject that hadn't received much attention. I could tell they felt a bit out of their comfort zone, so I suggested, "Take a guess." After more than a minute, one responded, "Thinking."

The answer didn't surprise me. This company had scaled through several critical transitions rapidly and hiring smart people was a priority.

I've found that thinking is valued in every company with which I've worked. It's fair to say that thinking is a prized attribute in America. There may have been a time when thinking was enough, but no longer. There is an abundance of smart people with great ideas, but consistent collaboration is more challenging and much more valuable.

When I asked them to describe what thinking is, the conversation became interesting. Their responses included planning, processing information, analysis, strategizing, judging, evaluating, prioritizing, and learning. This range of answers led me to be more curious, so I asked each to "think" about what percentage of their average day they spent thinking, and then write it down. Answers ranged from twenty percent to eighty percent.

Next, I asked them to reflect on their communal answers and share their observations. This is when they demonstrated vulnerability: a feeling of being uncertain, of not knowing.

In my work with management teams, this is an important threshold. I want to know if they can bear the discomfort of vulnerability. We can't access the deep learning we hope for without vulnerability. Since many executives have built their personas around being informed—"in the know"—I wondered how this first leap would go.

Rumination is the focused attention on the symptoms of one's distress and its possible causes and consequences, as opposed to its solutions.

The first person who spoke was Howard, the Marketing leader, who shared, "It 'feels' like I'm thinking all the time," he said slowly, "but I'm not doing the activities we described as 'thinking'. So, if I think I'm thinking, but I'm not, what am I doing?"

As our management team conversation continued, the group discovered that what they considered to be "thinking" was actually rumination. Rumination is the focused attention on the symptoms of one's distress and its possible causes and consequences, as opposed to its solutions. Both rumination and worry are associated with anxiety and other negative emotional states.

So, we shifted back to our original question, "What goes on inside of you?," and we parsed our "inside life" into pieces, like executives would if they wanted to analyze the parts of a problem. We continued this "thinking" because it seemed most comfortable to them.

Then we moved to feelings. I asked them what percentage of their average day they spent feeling, and this time their answers ranged from eight percent to one-hundred percent.

While the spread was significant, there was still one more category to cover: emotions. They were wising up, so before they would answer the "what percent" question, they wanted to know the difference between feelings and emotions.

Feelings tend to be short-term states that constantly flow through us, while emotions tend to take a longer time to subside. Because emotions cause subconscious feelings that, in turn, initiate more emotions, life can become a never-ending cycle of painful and confusing emotions that produce negative feelings, which cause more negative emotions without our ever really knowing why. Stuck feelings can become emotions.

Ruminating can be a doom loop—a potent buffer of mental activity that is governed by emotion—and is triggered by a relatively current set of feelings paired with historical thoughts associated with those feelings over a lifetime. Ruminating is the source of most of the tiredness I see, and it is the primary distraction leaders experience. As long as doom looping goes on, straightforward conversations become less possible and clear thinking is impaired.

Once they were comfortable with the emotion question, their answers ranged from ten percent to eighty percent. As they reflected on what they learned from one another, I heard these comments and I knew their awareness was growing:

- o "I am spending too much time ruminating due to stuck feelings and emotions."

- o "I have a large amount of stuck emotions that I am carrying around every day."

- o "I need to spend much more time feeling."

- o "Ruminating is occupying too much time and preventing action."

At times like these, I'm drawn to this simple Warren Bennis quote: "Leadership is the wise use of power. Power is the *capacity* to translate intention into reality and sustain it." Wisdom, power, and execution emanate from *within the capacity* of a leader, and the buffer of rumination impairs value creation.

Our body-mind is composed of approximately 70-100 trillion cells that make up every organ and the tissue that we most visibly notice. When you go to work, all of these cells are with you. Our body-mind, in a scientific sense, is a self-organizing system that automatically works to *survive*, but it doesn't know how to *thrive* unless we guide it. Any health threat, like a physical wound, virus, or bacteria, is immediately met by a corresponding and automatic health response. This reaction to disruption automatically restores balance.[4]

Humans are not biological robots; we live for meaning, and we are created to interpret every experience through the automatic question: "What does this mean?" Just as our body-mind automatically reacts to restore a healthy balance to our body so we can survive, this millisecond reaction is designed to do the same by assigning a meaning to each experience.

HOW RUMINATION STARTS
We each have a built-in "sense-making" capacity that operates continually. The more experienced a leader is, the more this capacity runs on autopilot. When an experience doesn't map with our own "felt needs" and expectations, you can imagine what automatically happens.

Scarcity is one of the feelings that arises when we don't feel our expectations are being met. It is often associated with money, but it usually has a much deeper source in the psyche— the place where all of our childhood experiences and wounds are invisibly stored. Thinking, feelings, and emotions are either in the service of scarcity or in the service of abundance. We avoid reality when we feel threatened.

I am sure we all know stories of how good people were unknowingly captive to automatic patterns of thinking, feeling, and behaving that led to costly unintended consequences. I find rumination in every company, and that's one reason engagement is statistically very low.

The brain is the most energy-hungry organ in the body, so when rumination captivates *attention*, guess where our energy goes? *Not* to thinking. Rumination and suffering are synonymous, and unless suffering can be brought into the light of relationship, rumination will flourish. I suspect that the lack of engagement and passion as shown in the Gallup studies is telling us that employee and manager "sense-making" capacities are running overtime. It seems that employees cannot make clear sense of their work, how they fit, and who cares for them, and neither can managers. But there is another way.

THE ANTIDOTE TO RUMINATION

Ted encountered this other way in one of our very first meetings. As a Vistage chair, I have monthly one-on-one meetings with each CEO in my group. Early in our relationship, Ted showed up fifteen minutes late. With Seattle traffic this wouldn't be surprising, but the fact that he acted like it hadn't happened was noteworthy.

Without a word about being late, he sat down and started giving me an update. I stopped him and asked, "Who else are you doing this to in your life?" When he looked confused, I said, "Showing up late without an apology." He paused, his face turned reddish, his eyes started to water, and he said, "My wife."

As I let his answer linger, the weight of his *automatic behavior* of being late seemed to gain traction. Then I asked, "What does this behavior say about you and the person you are standing up?" He hesitated, his eyes shifted down, and he slowly replied, "That I'm more important."

Ted's behavior was an automatic reaction to a need to feel important that had been lurking in his shadow. If you knew his childhood story, as I now do, it would be completely understandable. Even when the wounds of childhood trauma are tucked away, the emotional experience places chemical markers in the brain structure. The automatic reactions that their structure creates are always completely visible to those who can notice. Helping him get to know himself by reflecting on his life helped me embrace his reactions with compassion, which gave him a safe place to work on them.

Vulnerability is the ultimate source of real connection. Without it, our relationship would have been toast. Without vulnerability, we would maintain pretense.

Ted and I discovered that day that the work of *being present to reality is central to leadership*. Once Ted stepped into a vulnerable place of allowing others to help him see himself, he never looked back. Vulnerability is the ultimate source of real connection. Without it, our relationship would have been toast. Without vulnerability, we would have maintained pretense. Choosing to become vulnerable is the shortest path to minimizing rumination because it takes the fodder that's feeding the doom loop and brings it into the light.

Pretense is a posture that insulates a leader from discomfort, and it seems to correlate with the need to avoid reality; it's a reaction to a perceived threat. Pretense and posturing flourish in most company meetings, and effective meetings are really nothing more than purposeful conversations.

But, just as the desire to avoid pain is part of the human condition, for a leader, stepping toward discomfort without reacting is part of leadership. Most leaders, though, haven't had a space to practice, so being present with reality is very difficult. From the point that we identified Ted's pretense and began working to address it, Ted's progress was very rapid.

Are you getting the picture? With all the pretense and rumination going on, no wonder dealing with reality is so challenging and engagement is so low.

Conversations Are Space

A spoked wheel is a useful image for depicting the concept of working together—of genuine engagement. We can easily grasp the idea of each member of a team being a spoke that fulfills an invaluable function for the whole. However, I believe there is a deeper understanding that illuminates both where sustainability originates and the importance of leader awareness. Lao-tzu, in the *Tao Te Ching*, tells us:

"We join spokes together in a wheel,
but it is the center hole
that makes the wagon move.

We shape clay into a pot,
but it is the emptiness inside
that holds whatever we want.
We hammer wood for a house,
but it is the inner space
that makes it livable."[5]

Just as the hole in the center of the wheel is space, a conversation also is space, and, like the wheel, its purpose is to help us move forward. A conversation is meant to be useful, and we achieve this purpose with intention and structure. Creating space for important recurring conversations is critical because it helps everyone make sense, and rumination ceases.

Conversations form precious human energy into value or waste.

Conversations form precious human energy into value or waste. Throughout the book we will explore each of the nine management team conversations I have identified that are essential for sustainability and see them in action. I hope to help you understand how the interactions that take place within your management team space ultimately determine your company's ability to sustain value creation.

When the corrosive patterns that lurk in the shadows remain hidden, you and your team will always become sidetracked, squander energy, and lose momentum. Like sand slowly working its way into the gears of a fine watch, corrosive patterns can eventually convert a management team into passive role players who participate in an arduous dance for survival, leaving the owner with a nearly impossible burden to carry.

The *quality* of the conversation determines how useful it is, not the *quantity* of words. In every company, these conversations become more useful with practice. Every owner wants a sustainable management team, but very few have the experience to get there.

I believe the capacity of a management team and each of its members to practice and, ultimately, maintain these vital conversations is the framework for sustainability. As we move through these structures, I invite you to compare what takes place in your company today with what could be possible.

It All Works Together

When I consult with CEOs and owners, the desire they initially express most often is for more growth, and I understand why. Without growth, it's not possible to meet the needs of employees and customers over the long term. For the company to become sustainable, growth is essential. Yet a poorly initiated conversation about growth would simply divert scarce energy away from what makes growth happen.

Revenue and profit growth are by-products: they flow from *value creation*. When your *Your management team is the epicenter of your company.* company consistently delivers potent value, you attract customers.

Each of the conversations I have identified has a structure that can help you upgrade the quality of energy that flows from the management team through leader effectiveness into value creation, execution, and growth. Separating each conversation is helpful because it creates awareness, space to practice, and ownership for keeping the conversations and their quality in front of us. Initially, structure can feel constrictive, so bear with this.

FINDING THE THRESHOLD OF POSSIBILITY

At an early meeting of his management team cohort, Ted decided to share the story of his life, with all the bumps and bruises, from childhood on. Ted had shared his story with his friends in his Vistage CEO group but not with his management team.

Ted had come to understand that his self-knowledge was sponsoring integration, and with this, he felt more whole. He was more able to move thoughtfully toward his many difficult leadership challenges without reaction. He was responding to a deep longing (one that each of us has) to embrace the truth and find the resilience that lives within our essence—to bear with difficult things, to quit hiding, to walk humbly with inner uprightness. By doing his life audit work, Ted was coming to accept himself; and, by sharing this with his management team, he was becoming known—not the image that he wanted to project, but his true self that had been in hiding. By opening the doorway to vulnerability, Ted was inviting his management team to escape the doom loop of rumination.

Ted's *inner fluency* was growing, and now he wanted that for his management team. Inner fluency acknowledges that energy and information flow into us through our senses, but most of us don't understand the vital role our senses play. We have the five senses most people are familiar with—hearing, sight, smell, taste, and touch—and also the sixth sense: the signals from our heart, intestines, internal organs, muscles, and lungs. The seventh sense is being aware of memories, thoughts, emotions, beliefs, attitudes, longings, desires, intentions. And our eighth sense— our interconnections to others and the larger world in which we live, our relational sense.[6]

Management team meetings are the scaffolding where these insights emerge through lightly held rituals.

As we embrace our humanness with all of its strengths, limitations, and potential in the presence of others, we become more integrated and our capacity to bring these eight senses into awareness creates an inner stability that increasingly remains open and present with reality. Inner stability is what we need from each management team member.

The central impasse between achieving sustainability in your company and maintaining fragmentation is *management team coherence*—the quality of authentically forming a unified whole by cultivating a capacity to lead from the edge of the inside, through inner fluency. Management team meetings are the scaffolding where these insights emerge through lightly held rituals.

The idea of "impasse" is central to this book because impasses play a necessary role in every aspect of life and creation.

I often begin by showing a four-minute time-lapsed video of an acorn becoming an oak tree to the management teams I work with and through it they begin to understand and embrace the often stressful process of creation. The acorn, which is the seed that contains the full potential of a beautiful oak tree, is the first force. When it drops to the ground it encounters a second, denying force, the soil. For the seed to penetrate the ground, a third, reconciling force is necessary: sunlight. Together, all three forces generate a sprout, a fourth new force, which is the actualization of the latent possibility contained within the seed. The three forces—seed, ground, and sunlight—together open a whole new field or threshold of possibility.

Each of our lives cycle between impasse and threshold. If we stay in a closed loop of automatic reaction, we miss the threshold; but, if we can be with others who are growing in awareness and shining their light on what they see, the possibility of flourishing greatly improves.

Leading from the edge of the inside means you are becoming equally skilled at *noticing* and *regulating* your own feelings, thinking, and behavior while being present with those who are not. This stance is your key to allowing reality to materialize.

CHAPTER 2
THE ESSENTIAL CONVERSATIONS FOR VALUE CREATION

After 9/11, we all became more aware of how interdependent we are; but, after a while, we allowed our leaders to tell us that they could make us safe again, and we went back to sleep and embraced a false belief that this was their purpose. It's not.

Similarly, in business, it's not a management team's purpose to make sure everything is tame. The purpose of a management team is to sponsor value creation within the entire community we call a company. Everyone must have the opportunity to create and receive value, and this book is going to help you step into that purpose.

Each impasse that arises within this community we call a company is an opportunity. When a senior leader tries to insulate managers from difficulty (chaos), they are actually protecting themselves from the fierce feeling of vulnerability.

To most of us, withstanding an onslaught of questions without having answers can seem overwhelming. To cope, we avoid these conversations. In this situation, the purpose is to avoid feeling. These patterns can and need to change.

I challenged Dan, the COO of a company with which I worked, to ask his management team, "What would we do differently today if we knew that our biggest customer was going to be gone in twelve months?" Initially, he pushed back. When I asked him why, he said, "I don't want them freaking out, too."

This is an example of what it looks like when a management team lacks the capacity to fulfill its role. Dan was ineffective in allowing his staff to influence important decisions. In fact, his behavior was limiting the growth and development of his team members; it was blocking flow.

I can certainly relate to the volatile feelings Dan mentioned. Perhaps by stepping onto your personal viewing platform, you can, too. Dan had become fixated on avoiding these feelings, so he wasn't addressing the issues that ignited them either. He had moved into this pattern because he was guided by his unacknowledged commitment to avoid vulnerability. As a result, shaping energy into value creation wasn't possible. Visceral feelings emanate in the body-brain nervous system, and when we can be present with them, we can access a deeper part of us that supersedes logic. Dan's avoidance pattern had cut him off from this part of himself.

Dan's response to my question points to his state of being as it shifted between rigidity and chaos and back again. Because he blocked his scary feelings by staying in his stoic, rational mind, his capacity to develop himself and his team remained very limited. His feelings felt wild and untamed, and they were to be avoided at all costs. Dan was just trying to survive emotionally.

Everyone in your company knows how to survive, but it's up to the management team to model for and teach everyone how to thrive. When your company's leaders understand that *disruption is normal* and that their role is to shape energy into value or waste, you have turned an important corner.

What Is Challenging Your Management Team?

I've found a pattern of avoidance in most of the leadership teams I've guided. It's likely what's challenging your team as well. Why does avoidance happen? Each of us has a childhood story about surviving. It unconsciously shapes the flow of our adult thinking, feeling, and behaving, much like boulders in a fast-moving creek. These patterns form the adult energy that flows through us into value or waste.

Value Creation, not shareholder value, is the core of every company. Unless the way your company defines value creation is crystal clear, execution will be marginal, growth will be less than it could be, and labor costs will be too high.

In 1970, Milton Friedman declared to the General Motors management team that the purpose of a management team was to increase shareholder value. GM went on to underfund pension obligations, underfund research and development, and eventually require a government bailout. Clearly, this thinking comes from a place of scarcity. During the following decades, as the shareholder value paradigm was widely embraced and CEO pay became tied to share price increases, researchers noticed employee engagement eroding. Today, only around one third of US employees are engaged in their work.

Value Creation, not shareholder value, is the core of every company. Unless the way your company defines value creation is crystal clear, execution will be marginal, growth will be less than it could be, and labor costs will be too high. When value creation isn't clear and potent, micromanagement becomes necessary. This increases the number of employees and supervision costs while simultaneously decreasing quality.

Let's face it, the people who work in your company are either engaged or not based on whether the work they do serves their important purpose. When it does, work becomes meaningful and engagement improves.

Sustainability requires the mutual creation of value. Employees, owners, managers, suppliers, and their communities, as well as customers, must receive and create meaningful value. *A company becomes sustainable when value emerges with each human interaction.* Favoring customers and shareholders only insures that staff engagement will never spread throughout the company.

Rate of Adjustment

As you are starting to grasp the management team challenge, I want to pause to explain the concept of "rate of adjustment," which relates to how well a company or its parts adjust to disruption. If the internal rate of adjustment matches or exceeds the external rate of disruption, things should go well. Rate of adjustment is ultimately governed by the way a management team collaborates together and with others. Organic collaboration optimizes the rate of adjustment, while managed collaboration can create adjustments that require more adjustments.

My client, Richard, and his senior management team were high-energy optimists. Their company had grown from one line of business to multiple business units, and this was testing their ability to manage change. The first time I sat in on one of their executive meetings, I noted that their interactions were rapid, humorous, and safe. A well-established pattern kept each member in a role. Among those on the leadership team, I noticed some significant roles emerging. Debby, the CFO, and Lisa, the HR leader, were silent observers; Bill, the business development leader, provided sarcasm; Hugh, the IT leader, merely validated and expanded on what the CEO said; and Richard, the CEO, made sure the energy remained upbeat. The group seemed committed to avoiding silence.

I knew some foundational work needed to be done, so after a break, I asked, "How much change is underway in your company?"

As was their habit, words filled the air. They laughed about all the changes taking place, and it seemed that this helped calm their anxiety. I let the space be cluttered until they slowed down, and then I asked again, "How much change is underway in your company?"

This awkward space once again filled with humor, so I intervened once more, "I'd like you to let go of the humor and *stay with* the question: How much change is underway in your company?"

There was a pause, and a quiet space opened that allowed the quality of energy to shift. Then Stewart, the sales leader, who hadn't offered a word so far, said, "Too much." With his answer, the energy in the room changed from shallow, deflective humor to a quiet depth. They were ready to explore through conversation. Into this unusual space, Margaret, a division head, interjected, "I'd actually like to know how much change is underway. It seems overwhelming."

This conversation continued until Margaret volunteered to survey the company to see how many change initiatives were underway. At their next meeting, she presented a brief report identifying forty-one initiatives. More important, she discovered a corrosive, cancerous pattern: an attachment to drama.

> *Energy is transformed into waste when we try to prevent the interior experience of chaos by clinging to rigid, old patterns.*

Margaret found that throughout the company, change was launched with excitement, but the follow-through on new initiatives was only marginal. It seemed that when any new project encountered obstacles, employees' enthusiasm for the initiative waned, and it slid quietly to the back burner. While it appeared as if it were the poor closeout rate on initiatives that was stifling the company's ability to move forward, that wasn't actually the root cause.

An addiction to excitement is dangerous because it leads us to make choices that create more excitement that may not be in the best interests of the company long-term. In this case, Richard, the authority figure and CEO, had unconsciously become attached to excitement and drama. This was what was hijacking his management team conversations and converting limited energy to waste.

Energy is transformed into waste when we try to prevent the interior experience of chaos by clinging to rigid, old patterns. Richard's team shows what happens when we allow too much chaos. They avoided vulnerability, just like Dan in our earlier example; they just did it through humor. When management teams aren't vulnerable, they lack a resilient core; therefore, conversations don't have a place to grow. Teams then don't practice getting better; instead, they avoid risk.

Many management teams struggle to hold the entirety of this space until awareness grows through the practice of collaboration.

Martin Laird describes awareness well:

Our innumerable states of mind—thoughts, mood, and character—is an ever-changing pattern of weather . . . (our) awareness witnesses all of these changing patterns of weather as they move through our psychological terrain, changing as all weather does. Awareness itself is never awareness of some *thing*, yet by virtue of its simplicity, it grounds all things and is never separate from anything.[7]

He goes on to say that as weather is to a mountain, thoughts, ideas, distractions, and attachments are to awareness. Our intention is to get to a place where we allow these to flow through our awareness without grasping or identifying with them.

Feeling into Inner Awareness

Let's turn back to Dan for a moment. In his formative years, Dan had learned to avoid chaos by becoming stoic. But now his inner and outer world made the need to move forward critical.

He met individually with each member of the team and asked them the question: What would we do differently today if we knew our biggest customer would be gone in a year, and, telling them to thoughtfully prepare a response and come to a meeting with ideas. When they individually asked Dan what he thought they should do, he said, "I don't know. That's why we need to work this out together."

During the month surrounding this entire process, I gave Dan an assignment. I asked him to *notice* the kind of energy he *felt* in his body. Afterward, in our debriefing, he shared the following: "Before my initial one-on-one meetings, I felt fearful, like they would think I was overreacting. Leading up to the team meeting, I felt fear and anxiousness, but I also felt some excitement. I shifted from pessimism to optimism and back again. I felt tense. After, I felt relief and disappointment in myself. But then I realized they can go deeper than I thought. They shared some good ideas and I don't feel like I need to carry this alone."

This is where the cutting edge of integrity resides. The health of our integrity determines our inner strength and resilience. As you encounter outer world disruptions, stop and listen: when you do, these boulders will tell you where they are. As with Dan, it's our job to notice; to be aware.

How well team members accept responsibility for the state of their own inner being correlates to each management team's capacity to lead well. The feelings Dan described are related to the overall inner state we call vulnerability. While these are the feelings most of us have learned to avoid, they are also the feelings that the leadership journey calls us through. The management team exists to help us navigate the energetic currents of the inner and outer world of a company. By embracing our inner experience about the outer world, we become more able to shape energy into value creation.

The management team exists to help us navigate the energetic currents of the inner and outer world of a company.

A company senior management team is a wonderful place to work on this, and, as the rate of change and disruption throughout the world accelerates, I believe this work will become mandatory.

We choose to find our way into harmony as we learn to cultivate awareness. Awareness is always present. But, like Dan, most of us try to avoid chaos, so the wisdom that awareness gives can't guide us. We strengthen the inner ground of our being when we move through the states of rigidity and chaos by acknowledging our feelings. This is how a management team becomes sustainable. Wisdom never fails.

Dan's desire to control the conversations had come from a desire to avoid the experience of vulnerability, of not knowing. Staying rigid had been his go-to state. Dan's inner-fluency was young, but because he was starting to *notice* the flow, Dan was waking up to his interior life. His integrity was growing.

Conversations Are Structure

If you asked a third party to prepare a description of your company, they'd likely start by collecting data, looking at your website, and talking to your customers. This is an outside-in perspective that describes how your customer might initially see your company, but it doesn't tell us much about your company. To understand your company, you need to observe the quality and nature of the conversations that flow between your people.

Wherever each sits on the continuum between waste and value creation, conversations are, in fact, the lifeblood of your enterprise.

Conversations exist on a continuum. Some contribute in valuable ways while others create waste. Wherever each sits on the continuum between waste and value creation, conversations are, in fact, the lifeblood of your enterprise. They contain meaning and transmit energy and information.

I've discovered nine conversations that, to one degree or another, form the core of your enterprise. The quality and consistency of each one drives everything.

- The Value Creation Conversation

- The Execution Conversation

- The Growth Conversation

- The Leader Effectiveness Conversation

- The Management Team Coherence Conversation

- The Collaboration Conversation

- The Connection Conversation

- The Inner-Fluency Conversation

- The Work Conversation

The more willing you are to observe the feelings forming and flowing within you, the more you will be able to use these conversations to shape energy into *value*. If I only provided more information and knowledge about this, I'd be setting you up for more frustration. My intention with this book is to help you gain understanding, desire, and specific ways to practice.

Understanding emerges by combining information, knowledge, and personal experience, so I share stories of others and ask you to connect to your own similar experience—your personal viewing platform. When you do this, desire will also emerge. Once desire emerges, each conversation becomes a playful practice field for you and your management team. And the conversations build on one another, helping you progress through levels of sustainability. As you practice, you will grow your ability to have more and more meaningful conversations, and that accelerates value creation and growth. You can do this work in your management team meetings.

When you do the *work* of practicing, *inner fluency* (your deeper self-awareness and ability to speak from that place) grows, giving you greater capacity for more creative *connection* to yourself and others. This results in organic *collaboration* within the robust relationships of the management team. The team experiences *coherence*—their unity of purpose. As your team grows in coherence, it becomes a wonderful container that sponsors greater and greater levels of *leader effectiveness, execution, value creation, and growth*. Initially, you will begin with Value Creation, Execution, and Growth as the Outward-Moving Conversations.

But as your awareness expands, you move into and through the Together Conversations—the Leader Effectiveness and Management Team Conversations—and you achieve inner fluency, you will find yourself circling back around to the Outward-Moving Conversations with space for them to be more productive, more sustainable, and more organic.

By shifting these nine essential conversations from casual to intentional, we accomplish two important things.

First, we improve our ability to shape precious human energy into value creation, and if we keep at it, an abundance of value becomes available. Owners, employees, customers, suppliers, and the communities that sustain these people experience more abundance, too.

As we immerse ourselves in the conversational experience related to each of of the nine conversations we begin to rethink the idea of what a company is. The commonly held idea of what a company is does not explicitly include value creation as one of its purposes, yet, many companies need to increase their mediocre levels of value creation. A sense of scarcity is stressing the fabric of connection between employees, managers, and owners. Connection and collaboration are to value creation as sunshine is to a plant.

When each leader and employee learns that value creation is a company's purpose, and that *every interaction is intended to create some level of value*, the flywheel effect sets in: less and less energy is required to sustain greater and greater levels of value creation.

The second important point that we achieve when we shift the nine essential conversations from casual to intentional is that your team begins to practice these conversations on a regular basis. To achieve the flywheel effect, you have to practice. Imagine trying to accomplish one turn of a flywheel from a dead stop. This is how your management team will initially feel as they awkwardly practice these conversations. Think of this as an exercise.

Doing an exercise does not mean we need to feel a certain way afterward, or that we will feel the same way each time. In fact, each person on your management team will feel differently because our brains are wired differently. With these exercises you are strengthening your capacity to focus attention, to notice distraction, and to intentionally redirect attention. Different brain circuits control the dimensions of attention that sustain focus. Each of these conversations are training new circuits to sustain, notice, and redirect attention. Where attention goes, neural firing flows, and neural connection grows. The quality of attention correlates to the quality of the conversation.

Your old conversational patterns were activating well-worn neural networks. But, in just a few short minutes, this shift will start to activate important parts of your brain that have been inactive. This will feel like exercise. The fundamental elements of practice—sustaining, noticing, and redirecting—will grow stronger as your do it.

These conversations can generate an abundance of meaning, something we all desire, regardless of role. Yes, quality of meaning is what each of us tries to create through our work. Meaning-making is valuable and work is a primary source of meaning! These conversations upgrade meaning and make it measurable. You will learn how to measure meaning.

The body of words, symbols, and concepts operating within each of these conversations are stores of information and meaning. The more they are practiced the more likely they are to instantly activate a consistent quality of energy in each team member, regardless of distance. Effective culture is symbolized by vocabulary and shared meaning. Because these conversations shape the flow of energy and information into value creation, possibility and potential expand. Conversational potential is shaped by vocabulary and shared meaning and sustained through practice; therefore, view each conversation as a practice.

These conversations are educational. If you stay with them, they will upgrade the entire management team's knowledge of how your enterprise optimally works. This developmental experience accelerates personal and professional growth, which ultimately contributes to creating the bench strength you will need to scale. This is a mindset change.

CONVERSATIONS AS PLAY

Unfortunately, our modern-day culture seems to believe that play is only okay once the work is done. Play is often consigned to the realm of children, but even children these days are finding fewer spaces for play and playfulness. It seems that our survival operating system has even invaded the lives of our children, as they now see sports as a path to success and survival. Is play purely for play's sake a waste of time? It seems that many view a minute of play as a lost opportunity to get ahead.

Authentic play is spontaneous, and playfulness is a characteristic of a healthy management team. When you practice these conversations in a lighthearted way, you are certain to stumble and bumble your way into playfulness, so allow the disruption to create something new. Playfully moving from rigidity into chaos by embracing vulnerability accelerates movement into harmony, and harmony is the state where wisdom emerges.

The ritual of management team meetings around these conversations can create a safe place to gently move toward one another in the difficult challenges of life and leading. By practicing the few essential management team conversations I will lay out for you, you will automatically create more value. As you explore the mechanics of each conversation, notice the shift that takes place within you. Because these conversations are new to you, you may feel some level of frustration. The patterns you have established don't give up easily. You may initially feel like these conversations aren't very enjoyable, but—slowly at first—they begin to reshape the movement of energy through your management team. Feeling awkward during this initial phase is normal. Bear with these feelings, and they will provide value by upgrading the flow of energy. Turn this work into play!

A NOBLE PURPOSE

The scientific concept of *entanglement* attempts to describe reality at the quantum level, where everything is interacting with everything else to one degree or another. In this state, particles lose their individuality: what happens to one affects them all. This is similar to the reality of your company, and herein lies the opportunity. To harness this exponential power of reality, we must interact with noble purpose. As we do, we more effectively shape energy into value.

When management team members thoughtfully interact with each other through the nine conversations (after an initial period of awkwardly practicing the mechanics), flow emerges—they find their oneness. Without the conversations, decoherence sets in.

What is *decoherence*? Traditionally, most of us think that interactions with the outside world (which are also seeking to shape our energy) are the source of many problems. From the company's viewpoint, the outside world typically includes competitors, the economy, industry disruption, technology disruption, customer rate of change, family stress, and the physical and mental health of each staff member. These tend to pull your staff's energy in different directions and interfere with engagement and productivity. This is called "decoherence."

Coherence isn't a new idea. A seventeenth century Dutch scientist named Christiaan Huygens first noticed this effect while sick in bed. He had two pendulum clocks on his mantel and noticed that no matter how they were swinging when started, they would eventually synchronize. Eventually, they would find *their rhythm of oneness*. They seemed to self-organize.

Nature has somehow created and sustained an environment where flow naturally occurs.

Even more telling is that if you place two living heart cells from different people in a petri dish, even though they remain separate, they will find and maintain a third common beat. This biological fact shows how all things are invisibly related.[8] Nature has somehow created and sustained an environment where flow naturally occurs. We call this harmony, and all people are naturally inclined toward it.

While the clearing we create through conversation is both a space and a process, it also has spirit. While process can be taught, and certain kinds of clearings can technically be created, it is spirit that leads us into wisdom.

At this point you might naturally wonder, *What is spirit?* We could ask this question, but I don't think any of us could come anywhere close to an adequate explanation. Yet each of us, if we pause and acknowledge something deep within ourselves, knows what I'm talking about.

The reason is because Spirit is always present in us but mostly unacknowledged. If you observed my Vistage CEO group in action, words like vulnerable, gentle, curious, deep explorers, and fun would all come to mind. What might seem like work to some is play for them. These CEOs come together each month to work on their businesses and themselves and to playfully help each other like children. Their connection is vibrant. Value emerges through conversations.

While each member is clearly having a valuable experience, I doubt that any could articulate a precise value they received. In this group, as they give their gifts and practice getting better at giving, something magical always happens: value emerges well beyond anything they imagined.

A management team that lacks clear and noble purpose decoheres. While individuals can practice honing this skill or that, the entire management team cannot, until a noble purpose harnesses the power of collaboration.

When purpose is meaningful and clearly understood, coherent self-organization emerges, and long-term sustainability becomes possible.

What is the purpose of purpose? The purpose of a clock is not to measure time; it is to allow humans to coordinate their activity. Think about how clock-dependent we are in relation to our daily activities. Just like the clock, noble purpose invisibly pulls us toward the future in a coordinated way.

If purpose pulls us toward the future, and if we are unclear about purpose, our survival and comfort preferences prevail. This is what I see in many management teams. The environment is so filled with inner noise that deeply embedded patterns hijack coherence into distraction. Organic teamwork requires a noble purpose.

Purpose coheres the development and activity of the parts. When purpose is meaningful and clearly understood, coherent self-organization emerges, and long-term sustainability becomes possible. In other words, the spirit of the group draws the parts into self-organizing. The most noble purpose you can embrace is value creation. We will show you how to do this in the right spirit.

As you practice the conversations, play and wisdom will eventually emerge, but only when you are attentive to a noble, meaningful, and clear purpose.

A Place of Practice

I learned *about* business at college, specifically economics and marketing. These learnings created a frame of reference. When I joined Xerox, I received months of *training* on consultative selling and product knowledge. This training was a rigorous process— *and upgraded my frame of reference.* In my sales territory, I *practiced* consultative selling, and this is where I *developed* my craft.

While education tells us *about* something, training tells us *how to do* something. On the other hand, development is the *iterative process* of experimenting, adjusting, and experimenting again. Development is about trial, error, and reflection. Although having the framework for these conversations is educational, your management team needs to become a *place of practice* for the conversations to actually help you.

The conversations I lay out in this book can help you understand what a *practice* framework looks like. When you read through the descriptions of each, please pause and try to imagine what your company could become if each management team member were authentically *practicing these conversations*. If you will linger with this for a bit and learn to savor the possibilities, I trust you will discover an energy flow that can capture your imagination. Desire will emerge.

Since change is constant, you cannot practice without feeling vulnerable. While practice helps you eventually experience flow, practice, and vulnerability go hand in hand. Embracing the capacity to experience vulnerability is a core leader competency. Public practice is best. We learn humility when we realize we are incompetent. Humility is to a leader as sunlight is to a tree.

Just as practice needs to be part of the management team experience, practice is also part of the experience of each individual employee and customer. We practice developing the gifts we have been given, and the company is the place where practice can flourish, but only when we avoid denial.

Leading beyond the peaks into the troughs is challenging, yet the opportunity for others to help us understand ourselves is greatest here. When these experiences are accepted with humility, transformational growth is available.

CREATING INNER STRENGTH

Midway through my career with First Data, the management team decided to make a trip to Florida for a weekend of golf at TPC Sawgrass. Having never played, I declined, but the CEO insisted I go. To make matters worse, he insisted I join his foursome so that he could offer some pointers.

As you can imagine, this certainly was a memorable experience (I lost twenty-nine balls over two rounds). As I recall, this was probably my first professional experience with humiliation.

Our next golf outings took us to Spyglass and Pebble Beach, and these were my last outings for twenty years. Golf had become a symbol of my inadequacy and a source of separation, but with the wisdom of a proper practice frame of reference, it could have been a developmental experience.

The Practice Experience

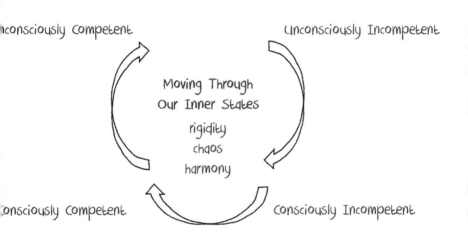

Unconsciously Competent

Unconsciously Incompetent

Moving Through
Our Inner States

rigidity
chaos
harmony

Consciously Competent

Consciously Incompetent

The Practice Frame of Reference Illustration above shows us how we move through our Inner States. Before I ever played golf, I was *unaware of my incompetency* because I never had reason to think about it. When I first played, I moved into a state of *chaos* by becoming aware of how incompetent I was in comparison to seasoned golfers, and this chaos was terrifying. Being *conscious of my incompetence* in the presence of others shook me to my core. In other words, this experience disrupted my survival operating system—the one that supported the way I needed to see myself. Clearly, I had over-identified with success.

Each time we start the journey of *practice,* disruption occurs. Although disruption might be shocking, it's vital. To one degree or another, disruption always precedes transformation. I'm told that the rudder on an aircraft carrier is such a large surface that, prior to turning, a series of small electrically controlled tabs unfold from its surface to disrupt the water pressure and create space for the rudder to move into. When we experience disruption, space opens for something new to emerge. In a later chapter, we will learn to navigate the inner state of chaos, but for now, just accept that it's necessary.

Something magical happens inside every management team with which I've worked when members are all demonstrating the chaos of practice: fun emerges. In one sense, it's like being kids again. Yet, if one member of the team, including the CEO, resists the movement toward chaos, the entire team pulls back into their survival identity shell like a turtle under attack.

IMPASSE IS A GIFT
When everyone views a company's purpose as value creation, we can use each impasse to strengthen community. Impasse is the source of all transformation. Companies can become communi-

ties if we allow impasse to serve its purpose. Each impasse invites us to be more attentive to our inner states and our connection to each other through our common future. This allows self-organizing to flow through Collaboration, Management Team Coherence, Leader Effectiveness, Execution, Value Creation, and Growth.

If we believe the media, it seems we have become accustomed to thinking about what we can get or how to take advantage of a situation, but I find that most people aren't actually this way. Most people seem to want to be respected and acknowledged for their contribution. Under this desire is a deeper question: "What is my unique gift, and where can I freely give it?"

Absent the energy this question forms, another question takes its place: "What can I get?" This is a source of decoherence within the individual, the management team, and the company. When we give up on our gift-giving design, we become someone other than who we really are. We quietly slip on a mask to survive, and we disengage. Disengagement is a management team's enemy, and a management team's invisible conversational patterns have unknowingly created this beast.

However, within a gift-giving environment, company growth is organically governed by value creation. Our gifts are creative gifts, and they allow us to participate uniquely in the ongoing process of creation. When value creation isn't strong, it just means we have misaligned the gift people can uniquely give with the role they presently serve in support of purpose.

Employees whose work has separated them from their gift ultimately become noticeably disengaged. Leaders know when work is no longer energizing someone, yet because they don't have the framework we are describing, they allow themselves to ignore the cues in the interest of time.

A small group of people operating in their gift will rapidly grow their company until the number of people working outside their gift counterbalances momentum. When this happens, energy is drawn into recurring problem solving and diverted from value creation. To a large degree, this insidious pattern sets the limits of growth.

As a management team practices the conversations, the "give, receive, and give again" environment forms and reforms into a value creation community, which is the highest purpose a company can serve.

THE SPIRAL OF GROWTH

As a management team practices the conversations, the "give, receive, and give again" environment forms and re-forms into a value creation community, which is the highest purpose a company can serve. Just as rigidity, chaos, and harmony are the states of being that exist within each of us, coherence and decoherence are the normal rhythms of a company. Contrary to what most leaders expect, value creation and growth flow in a spiral pattern over time, both for individuals and for the company.

Gift-giving in the service of a greater common purpose forms the basis for coherence and decoherence. As you will see with the "Spiral of Growth" illustration that follows, the upward movement of growth—for the company and each person—is always followed by an adjustment because of the limits people encounter. But please note that even though each coil contains ascent and descent, the coils carry us into a spiral of growth overall when the peaks and the troughs are joined together. Both the highs and the lows form who we are. If we resist the lows and cling to the highs, we exit the natural flow of the spiral of growth. Low points

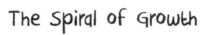

The Spiral of Growth

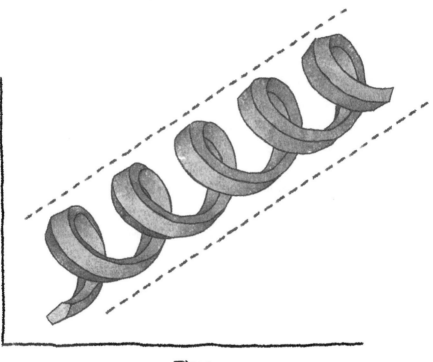

Time

can help us begin to see the ways we unconsciously contributed to the current state. This is how we develop our reflective capacity.

In one sense, the solid ground of leadership is depicted in our model of the spiral. This model is designed to help you assess (reflect on) how real your management team conversations are. We start by bringing this into awareness. To do this, a better understanding of practice is helpful. Simple practice rituals can transform consciousness, and over time, your capacity to hold the "field of awareness" improves.

The Nine Essential Conversations

Productive business conversations can feel subversive because unanswered questions are an inevitable, if not necessary, byproduct. Questions get people thinking, and real thinking, at the management team level, can be uncomfortable because we initially don't know the answer. Good questions open the door to fresh possibility. Staying with these questions until they yield answers requires inner strength and good structure. This ensures the patterns of interaction help form energy into value. This is their ultimate purpose!

I've noticed that most CEOs have a strong attachment to just one of the conversations. To become sustainable, all the conversations need to be practiced, and over time, this is possible. As we explore the context for these conversations, a few things are probably becoming clear. Scaling a company is challenging for a variety of reasons. You may be sensing within you a growing understanding of the commitment required of each leader. Also, you might just now be beginning to see how conversations are the cornerstone of your company. Conversations shape all the individual choices that channel raw energy into value or waste. When managed well, all conversations are personal because they create meaning. Addressing them reliably isn't something most leaders have learned how to do. Evolving in this art as a team can become playful.

You are also probably starting to be curious about the unique, invisible patterns that block you and your team, that prevent you from scaling and having a mature management team, and that keep you from becoming a more sustainable company.

The following nine conversations are initially challenging, but an awareness of them can be safely cultivated within the management team. You can experience transformation

When managed well, all conversations are personal because they create meaning.

together and rise above the insidious invisible patterns that have historically created waste. This is how you create a sustainable point of differentiation for your company.

1. THE VALUE-CREATION CONVERSATION

Commerce is as old as humanity—it's all about trade and exchange. With intense competition and the accelerating needs of customers, exchange has become much faster and the complexity of offerings has become greater. Clarity around your value-creation strategy allows your company to become fast, efficient, and scalable. Without it, scaling can become a costly repeating experiment.

2. THE EXECUTION CONVERSATION

The Execution Conversation specifically describes what is involved in *delivering* on a potent value-creation strategy. You may see some creative tension between leaders as they collaborate on this.

3. THE GROWTH CONVERSATION

Your company grows when it expands beyond the constraints of three limitations: the potency of your customer offering, the number of available customers, and the quantity and quality of your customer interactions. When you view each of these three constraints through the questions in that chapter, they will lead you into reality. Straightforward logic and factual analysis of readily available information provide clear direction for this conversation and strengthen decision-making.

4. THE LEADER EFFECTIVENESS CONVERSATION

The Leader Effectiveness conversation focuses on behavioral expectations of the management-team members. This is not a job description. This conversation powerfully transforms and shapes the management team patterns that create waste or value. It helps each member improve the contribution they make to the team, and it promotes coherence.

5. THE MANAGEMENT TEAM COHERENCE CONVERSATION

The management team is the epicenter of your company and it's the container where all these conversations shape energy. If you improve the team's ability to navigate the conversations and the resulting vulnerability, it creates coherence. While we offer no specific structure for this conversation, you will find that practicing all the other conversations creates coherence.

6. THE COLLABORATION CONVERSATION

Collaboration is to management what a gardener is to a garden. Scaling a company is primarily about pruning, fertilizing, tilling the soil, planting new seed, watering, composting, and weeding. When this is done with intention, growth and profitability result.

By growing the collaborative capacity of your management team, organic growth sets in. The Collaboration Conversation provides a framework for tending the garden. Each of our conversations is a collaboration generator.

7. THE CONNECTION CONVERSATION

High-quality connection between management-team members creates the fertile ground of organic collaboration. Connection grows through vulnerability, and vulnerability helps each member find their fit. When each member fits well, organic collaboration soars. The Connection Conversation creates a framework that helps each member become more connected.

8. THE INNER-FLUENCY CONVERSATION

As we encounter the inevitable disruptions and setbacks associated with leading, our inner state moves through feelings of chaos, rigidity, and harmony. If these are not properly tended, value creation becomes sidetracked. The Inner-Fluency Conversation provides a language that management team members can use to help themselves and each other navigate these intense inner currents.

9. THE WORK CONVERSATION

Becoming a centered leader requires *work*, and none of these conversations are going to be successful without you and your team working at them. Through practice we strengthen the ground of our being; and, as this occurs, our ability to help others navigate their powerful inner currents grows. The Work Conversation isn't a singular conversation you will have. It is a subtext, an ulterior motive if you will, for each of the other Essential Conversations. It is an internal conversation that identifies the practices that support the inner journey. These practices, when embraced by the management team, ultimately turn work into play.

I find that most management team members haven't thought much about how a business actually works; their frame of reference is feeling-oriented. Their mindset has been developed through the lens of their own discipline: sales, operations, finance, technology, and HR, to name a few. As you practice each of the conversations your mindset will shift. Your understanding of how a business actually works becomes simplified.

With this overview in mind, we shift from the conceptual to the experiential by sharing the stories of real leaders and their patterns. As you explore the next chapter, try to compare your own experience and patterns by creating a personal viewing platform. Rise above the information and reflect on how you and your management team compare.

CHAPTER 3
THE OUTWARD-MOVING CONVERSATIONS

Raymond, the CEO/owner of a rapidly growing firm, had taken a small company on the brink of collapse and driven compounded annual growth to thirty-five percent for three years by injecting a highly compensated sales team into the company. During this time, Raymond's anxiety was high, but he didn't know its source.

As I began working with him and his team through what I call the "Outward-Moving Conversations," I noticed that his team deferred to him whenever tension arose, but neither Raymond nor his team possessed the inner capacity to stay with the challenge (and the opportunity) this approach to conflict presented.

Oddly, given his obvious success, Raymond held a lot of fear that he tried to diffuse by accelerating growth. In one of our meetings, Nathan, the CFO, mentioned that execution was in trouble and that the rate of growth needed to slow until execution was stronger. All of five minutes was consumed by this comment because Raymond, in his addiction to growth fueled by a fear of failure, couldn't tolerate slowing down. A few months later, the CFO resigned. When execution collapsed, layoffs ensued, employee trust disintegrated, and the company's brand became tarnished.

This company had been collecting Customer Net Promoter Scores (cNPS) for years but was unwilling to address the hard questions the responses were indicating. For more than eighteen months, cNPS results had been telling Raymond that execution was wobbly. Like the final rotations of a top as its momentum deteriorates, Raymond and his management team were seeing increased instability and were simply trying to survive.

Unfortunately, it took a near collapse before Raymond could acknowledge that he had driven growth without paying attention to value creation and execution. Why did this happen?

Raymond had been a very successful sales leader with two large corporations, but he had never worked on the execution or value-creation side, and, frankly, neither company was good at creating clarity. Raymond unconsciously believed: *Sell what you can create in your mind, and operations will deliver.* This limiting belief, this mindset, created an attachment to growth at any cost.

Raymond was attached to a high-powered sales mentality. After the collapse, when he began looking for a chief operating officer, I asked him to draw up a success profile of his ideal candidate so we could discuss it. This helped Raymond realize that by leaving value-creation questions unanswered, he had sabotaged execution. Solid execution stands on the shoulders of a well-defined value-creation strategy.

In a strong, coherent management team, each leader takes ownership of an Essential Conversation—a COO typically owns the Execution Conversation, the sales leader takes on the Growth Conversation, and Value Creation is optimally owned by a senior marketing or business development leader. Raymond had been retaining ownership of all three, but he now wanted to let go too quickly. His addiction to speed was too powerful. Part of my work with him was to help him realize that, before making rapid changes, he needed to do some inner work to identify and shift away from old, unproductive patterns.

In many privately owned companies, value creation becomes lost while growth and execution attract energy. The normal diagnostic progression is that when growth slows, management teams or CEOs examine their execution. The first time value creation gets addressed is well after growth has slowed. This is too late.

Most privately owned companies don't have a methodology for insuring that value creation remains robust. In fact, in my experience, value creation often exists only as a feeling. When that feeling is converted to logic that is supported by a key metric and held by the management team as vital, traction dramatically improves and so does management team coherence.

By creating three separate conversations, each with a designated owner on the management team, we develop the management team, create a diagnostic process, and insure continuous improvement.

Each conversation is a collaboration generator. Collaboration always starts with one important unanswered question that is uniquely relevant to your company management team. As you collaborate through these conversation models, try to create a personal viewing platform by imagining how your management team would navigate the conversation. Frame it with an important question that emerges for you. As you stay in your imagination, how do you see your team functioning? Are they confident and able to articulate concise answers, or are they awkward and uncomfortable? Now imagine your own presence, your feelings, and your ability to facilitate the conversation. What do you see? Are you able to stay with the tension and allow it to do its work? Do you sense a tendency to avoid tension?

These Outward-Moving Conversations will feel the most familiar to you as they are common conversations within company operations. They may feel tedious because they can become rote and routine, yet doing them effectively is what leads us into more challenging—but productive—territory. It's my hope that by providing the framework for these conversations, you can choose to playfully practice them so you can be ready to turn inward later.

Each story I share in this chapter is intended to serve as a gateway to your personal viewing platform. Try to imagine the interior journey of emotion and feeling and the outer experience of being with your team as the authority figure. As important questions surface, imagine yourself in the story.

The Value Creation Conversation

In a management team meeting, David, the senior leader of a multidivisional company, asked Ethan, a division leader whose growth was marginal, to explain his value-creation formula. As Ethan awkwardly filled the space with words. David interrupted and asked, "What part of what you just said does your customer value?" When he again described what he "felt" they valued, the problem came into the clearing. Ethan's mindset—his frame of reference—wasn't value creation.

As a division leader, Ethan should have been able to succinctly communicate the customer problem his product and service addressed. Identifying the felt need is a key factor in your company's value-creation formula. When that is not clear, it's nearly impossible to improve. It's even more difficult to evaluate the leader and staff responsible for value creation, so accountability deteriorates.

The creative flow of energy within a company needs to remain strong; but, where there's no clear formula, creative energy has no place to work. Creative energy and innovation begin to flow with the desire to address your customers' problems, and this is how your staff finds meaning. Designing a solution to a problem always creates value. In fact, consulting companies primarily exist because they facilitate conversations that uncover problems.

Stop for a moment and imagine how you might have answered David's question. Most leaders of privately owned companies can't do what David did because they don't have the knowledge and the inner wherewithal to create the space for a question like this to linger. His question created tension, as all good questions do. Even with knowledge, many management teams don't know how to hold the inner tension—the place where silence replaces easy answers and quick fixes.

Each story I share in this chapter is intended to serve as a gateway to your personal viewing platform. Try to imagine the interior journey of emotion and feeling and the outer experience of being with your team as the authority figure. As important questions surface, imagine yourself in the story.

Feeling awkward—not knowing—is the challenge of vulnerability. Ethan simply could have said, "I don't know," and asked for help. In doing this, he could have created value by opening the door to growth, but it would have required exposing his vulnerability. By trying to cover his inadequacy with words, he sponsored decoherence. On the other hand, if David had asked Ethan to provide an update on the projects that drove revenue, he would have excelled because

Value creation is always at the core of every company.

his ascension into divisional leadership was through his success in leading projects. He had a unique ability to keep things on track, and he felt alive when doing so. This was his gift, but it was holding him and the company back.

As David's story demonstrates, lack of knowledge is one part of the problem. Beyond not knowing his value-creation formula, Ethan's own inner knowledge was very limited.

Having the inner wherewithal to stay with the conversation, question by question, is vital, as is the ability to say, "I don't know". Each conversation creates an opportunity to hold a vulnerable place of practice, a place to acknowledge what you don't know and to ask for help.

As we lay out the structure for the Value Creation Conversation, we are trying to encourage clarity so that knowledge and practice can follow.

WHERE VALUE CREATION BEGINS

As I have already stated, Value creation is always at the core of every company. Unless it's clear, execution will be marginal, growth will be less than it could be, and labor costs will be too high. To one degree or another, someone on your management team currently drives your Value Creation Conversation. I've found that the mechanics around this conversation are usually fuzzy. If you have multiple business units in your company, having someone who drives value creation in each is critical. Knowing who owns this conversation is vital because without a specific description of the expectations, value creation will remain fuzzy, and fuzziness leads to waste.

In most mid-market companies, people don't know who is supposed to sponsor a given conversation. In fact, the company owner often unconsciously carries the burden of owning all the important conversations, and none of them receives the attention they need. They all become sidetracked because no one person can be expected to engage in all of these conversations well. Each conversation should have one owner at the management team table if possible. If that is not possible, do your best to allocate the conversations to those on your team that appreciate structure.

By reconceptualizing the nature and relationship between value creation, execution, and growth, and providing separate and distinct conversations for each, we become clear, and clarity creates kindness. The mechanics outlined here offer you the opportunity to upgrade ownership through practice.

Though these conversations are interdependent and build on one another, we can accelerate our understanding by separating them. This sets in motion a methodology for improvement through practice. By having a key metric, we maintain visibility across the management team, and this supports the Leader Effectiveness Conversation, which we'll delve into shortly.

When a leader owns this conversation, he/she is expected to make sure the entire management team grows in their ability to contribute. Without clear ownership, execution deteriorates. With effective ownership, the execution team's conversations can create innovative ways of delivering on the Value Creation formula. The most strategic process for every company is the *Value Creation formula and the conversation that supports it.*

As the following illustration makes clear, the Value Creation Conversation is straight forward. It is easy to understand intellectually, makes common sense, and has been tested, as indicated by the thousands of companies that have mastered it. One widely accepted metric is used to track it: the cNPS.

While the Value Creation Conversation is widely used in most major companies, most mid-market companies haven't mastered it, so the way many teams engage around value creation squanders energy. By following this model, you can rapidly accelerate how quickly your team becomes effective.

Through better managed conversations, David's entire team recognized that although the strategy was clear, it was

The Value Creation Formula

Specific customer problem(s) targeted?

Detailed description of your solution(s)

Key customer metric(s) impacted

Exactly how your solution impacts this metric

Describe channels and how they are used

Describe customer segment, characteristics, and quantity

The Emotional Experience of Your Customer (cNPS score trend) impotent, and there was no way forward. David's value creation strategy for his division didn't create adequate value and unless they could find a way to increase the potency of their products and services, margins would erode.

When David's management team reengaged with each other around the conversation, they developed a full Value Creation formula in a much more thoughtful way and, a short time later, everyone understood.

In a later meeting with David, the conversation turned to the possibility of closing this division and having the talented staff join another growing division where their energy could be used to create value again.

David demonstrated his ownership of the management team space and his expectations about who owns value creation. But a few years earlier, he couldn't have done this. The patterns that were still hiding in the shadows at that time would have side-tracked his ability to own the management team space.

By having a well-documented and stable formula, execution can become efficient. By anchoring value with customer Net Promoter Score, you can become more certain. If, over time, cNPS shows deterioration, you can return to your Value Creation formula to examine it and preempt a decline in growth.

The value-creation strategy shapes the Execution Conversation. Execution includes the people, processes, systems, and equipment that deliver your specific Value Creation formula profitably through your channels to your specific customer segment.

The Execution Conversation

Gordon, the owner of several franchise stores, launched his business many years ago by investing in a strong national brand. With this, he secured a solid, reliable, and time-tested Value Creation formula and a network of peers to share data with and learn from.

For most of his employees, this was their first job, and Gordon embraced this as an opportunity to develop character and meaning in their lives through work.

I first met with his management team because they were frustrated with an inability to grow faster. Although a lack of growth was the presenting issue, it became clear that his staff's ability and willingness to deliver their strong Value Creation formula was inconsistent. Their inability to grow was caused by inconsistent execution, so we entered the Execution Conversation.

Because they were a franchisee within a reputable national brand, the Value Creation formula with its metrics and reporting was robust and crystal clear to all. So, as we attempted to stay with the Execution Conversation, it became apparent that a severe limitation to bench strength had been in place for years. While working with Gordon, the CEO, and Ralph, the COO, I noticed that it was hard for them to stay with the Execution Conversation long enough to identify the root cause of their stagnation. They were constantly being sidetracked, and it became clear that this was a long-standing pattern of waste.

Through the development of this conversation, we uncovered weakness from the store supervisory level up through the regional management team. While the COO would normally own this, it seemed that an insidious pattern of making sure no blame landed on anyone kept them from facing reality. No one actually owned the Execution Conversation.

As is often the case, Ralph had partnered with Gordon in the beginning to bootstrap their company by doing whatever needed to be done. Ralph ruminated on what to do about store-level management turnover, but he never clearly asked for help. You can imagine the impact this was having on employee engagement and costs and how this shadow pattern influenced their team.

For the better part of two years, this frustrating pattern maintained its hidden grip on the senior team. Finally, when two above-store leaders resigned and pointed a finger at Ralph's micromanaging behavior, a crisis emerged that Gordon decided not to waste, and this helped Ralph step into another role.

With nearly two-thirds of employees reporting feeling disengaged, it's no wonder so many owners struggle for so long to create a sustainable company and why the burden of ownership becomes so onerous.

When wasteful patterns are allowed to linger, employee engagement slides. Unless this is corrected, micromanagement sets in—exactly the case with Ralph.

After Ralph stepped into a non-supervisory role, Gordon noted that Ralph seemed lighter and more able to connect. I suspect that, secretly, he had wanted to let go for some time, but his sense of responsibility and his lack of a helpful frame of reference prevented vulnerability from doing its work.

WHY EXECUTION MATTERS

When I first encountered Gallup's survey data around employee engagement that I wrote about in Chapter One, I tried to understand what was driving costly levels of disengagement. With nearly two-thirds of employees reporting feeling disengaged, it's no wonder so many owners struggle for so long to create a sustainable company and why the burden of ownership becomes so onerous. Gallup concluded that employees' managers were the key determinant for their level of engagement, and I concur. Beneath this general statement, though, is knowledge that can change the way you lead.

Engaged employees use discretionary effort to accomplish things that are meaningful to them, and unengaged employees don't. Unengaged employees need very close supervision, while engaged employees don't.

The reasons employees give for lack of engagement are that they do not have clear performance expectations or that they don't receive the necessary training, education, and leadership support. We all know how much supervision employees need when their norm is not knowing specifically what's expected. Without knowing what's expected, an employee is robbed of learning, impact, and earned advancement—what Maslow labeled "self-actualization" and what Victor Frankl called *meaning*.

Once again, I invite you to use Gordon and Ralph's story as a way to enter your personal viewing platform. Try to imagine how your company would function with one hundred percent of your people engaged. Clearly, if we can find a way to improve staff engagement, we can establish a strong and very durable point of differentiation.

Execution is where most of your people expend their time and talents, initially with the hope of having impact and discovering meaning. When a clear, durable Value Creation formula is in place, the execution teams can rev up their creative engines.

The Execution Conversation is about creating a durable way of delivering the Value Creation formula while continually increasing employee engagement.

As this model shows, execution starts with a detailed understanding of the Value Creation formula. I call this the essence of your offer. The execution team develops a detailed plan that includes processes and support, technical and financial performance, and customer interaction with your people and processes, all with a focus on creating a strong emotional experience for your customer.

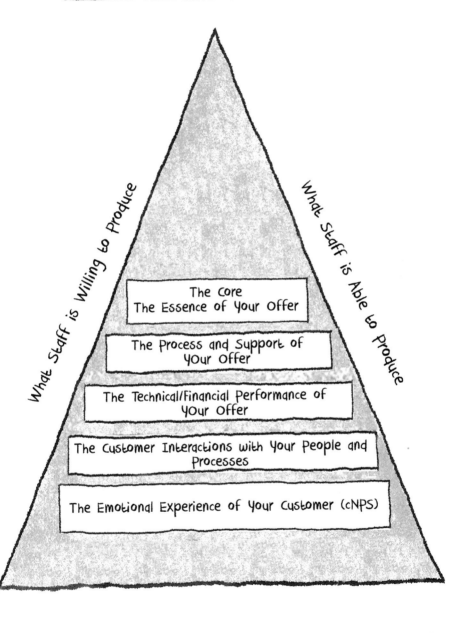

The Execution Conversation

What Staff is Willing to Produce

What Staff is Able to Produce

The Core
The Essence of Your Offer

The Process and Support of
Your Offer

The Technical/Financial Performance of
Your Offer

The Customer Interactions with Your People and
Processes

The Emotional Experience of Your Customer (cNPS)

While all of this is very straightforward intellectually, the next dimension—what your people are willing and able to do—adds a level of complexity that most mid-market leadership teams stumble and bumble their way through.

While most privately owned companies are able to grind through this process to create acceptable execution, many struggle to optimize what their staff is willing and able to produce, which leaves them unable to scale. I've noticed that leaders like Ralph stay for a very long time within the execution part of the company and often stagnate, which leads to a lack of future execution leaders. Without a crop of new leaders bringing fresh, innovative eyes to the Execution Conversation, scaling is nearly impossible.

Turning to your personal viewing platform, what is the emotional experience of your customer, and how is it tracked? What impact does this data presently have on your Execution Conversation? Can your execution team clearly articulate the essence of your offer accurately and with detail?

Even though growth, or the lack of it, is often the presenting issue for management teams, execution and value creation are the source of growth and must be clarified first. With this in mind, we will explore the Growth Conversation.

The Growth Conversation

Sharon was a savvy, time-tested leader, and her status within her industry was exemplary. She had grown and scaled several companies successfully. I was impressed that throughout the layers of leadership within her large organization, everyone seemed to possess precise knowledge about the number of available customers that could purchase their product and service at a price that provided a profit for the company. They had worked long and hard to execute well on the commoditized Value Creation formula that was standard across their industry. Their Execution Conversations were vigorous, as were their Value Creation Conversations.

I am sharing Sharon's story because it shows what's possible even when a product or service is commoditized; regardless of desire, there is no way to sustain a significant advantage through your Value Creation strategy. In her industry, maintaining and executing on a strong Value Creation formula is simply a requirement that all companies must meet. There is very little opportunity, over the short- or medium-term, to sustain a competitive advantage through superiority.

WHAT REALLY DRIVES GROWTH

Although Sharon's management team realized that their products and services had long been commoditized, they nevertheless achieved year-over-year compounded growth of more than fifteen percent by creating exceptionally high-quality customer interactions.

Customers purchase products or services with a belief that it will make their life better, more enjoyable, or less frustrating. These are emotional wants and needs. To the degree that these are met or unmet, growth becomes possible or difficult. While the foundation for growth is the potency of your offering, as the following model shows, three dimensions together form the constraints that limit or empower growth. These constraints should become the focus of all Growth Conversations. In the chapter on collaboration, we will share how important these questions are. In this model, potency of offering forms the foundation. The offering (your product or service) is potent when your Value Creation formula is strong and your staff is executing it well. But potency by itself isn't enough. If we assume there are enough customers who are willing to buy your offering at a price that

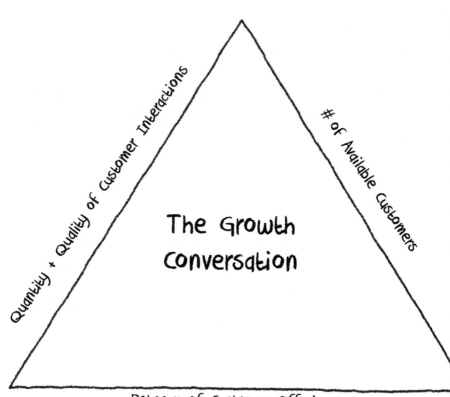

includes a profit for you, the factor that determines your rate of growth is the quantity and quality of your customer interactions.

The culture Sharon's management team ultimately developed and sustained attracted hundreds of the most professional people in their commoditized industry. The purpose of this culture was to recruit, support, and retain professionals with a desire and capacity for *connection*.

Over time, through the practices that I'll share later, this team started to offer themselves in fresh and revealing ways. Ultimately, this paved the way for deeper and deeper levels of connection and, to no surprise, started organic collaboration.

They discovered what few others have mastered—the importance of connecting, first to each other, and then to customers and referral sources. During their management team meetings, they made creating value for each other their normal, default behavior for every interaction. This taught them skills that they used throughout the company to help spread connection. The quality and quantity of their customer interactions were superior to their competitors, and they were committed to maintaining that edge by creating a container where they practiced connection. As you enter this Growth Conversation, I invite you to climb back onto your personal viewing platform and imagine how you and your team would answer the *number of available customers* question. Would it be precise? Is it kept up-to-date? Would the answer be segmented accurately to show only those who would buy at a profit? How would the team answer the *quantity and quality of customer interactions* question? Are specific and reliable facts available? Are reliable processes in place to support your intentions. And, can your customer-facing staff clearly articulate the potency of your offering (your Value Creation formula)? Finally, imagine yourself as the authority figure trying to facilitate conversations around each of these questions. How would you feel? How would you behave?

Further questions for your Growth Conversation:

- Are we measuring the potency of our offering over time with our Customer Net Promoter Score?
- What is the trend?
- How do we know this for certain?
- Specifically, how many valid customers are available today; what is the trend?
- How do we segment possible customers?
- What is the quality and quantity of our customer interactions?
- How do we define the highest-quality customer interactions? Is there a model staff member who can set the standard. Can we identify examples to learn from?
- Is there something beyond this kind of interaction?
- Are the answers we are providing facts or feelings?

The answers you receive will help make your Growth Conversations more productive and encourage goal setting.

Shifting from Outward to Inward

By separating value creation, execution, and growth, we gain clarity, which ultimately is kindness. Yet I hope you see that by doing this, each of the other conversations become more powerful; they are interdependent.

As you let this suggested list settle in, you might be tempted to dismiss the simplicity of this conversation, but remember that the Value Creation Conversation and the Execution Conversation determine the potency of your offering. The Growth Conversation must be established with facts. Growth is a requirement, so don't trust your gut. Without current facts, there is no long-term future for staff, owners, customers, or communities.

As we move into the next section—the "Together Conversations" that focus on Leader Effectiveness and Management Team Coherence—I challenge you to consider leading with intention by answering these questions: *How effective have I been as a leader? Can learning to master these conversations help me be intentional about my development?*

CHAPTER 4
THE TOGETHER CONVERSATIONS

The seeds of a multigenerational family company I began working with were initially sewn by a hard-working, opportunistic entrepreneur, as is often the case. Now, it had managed to scale well beyond the founder into a much more durable enterprise with multiple business units. The family maintained ownership but had also been able to attract and retain good managers from outside.

Avery, the founder's son, was full of positivity, and you might describe him as a bit of a cheerleader. This wouldn't be unusual considering he had progressed in his career through sales leadership.

Avery thrived on the recognition associated with success, and, by making small technology enhancements to improve customer value, Avery's business unit shined. As profit and revenue grew, his star rose within the company. However, while the potency of his unit's offerings remained strong, a subtle but very powerful impasse had been developing. It festered, hidden beneath the glitter of growth and profitability until there was no way to avoid it.

When I met the CEO, Don, I could tell he was angry. His CTO, Burton, had told him that an implementation within Avery's unit was behind schedule, and his team seemed unresponsive when queried.

Whenever resistance shows up regarding execution, I become curious about what the Employee Net Promoter Scores (eNPS) are, so I asked Don about Avery's unit. With frustration on his face, he commented, "the lowest in the company." When we looked further into employee comments, it became clear that Avery's team felt manipulated and overwhelmed by him. Their willingness and ability to execute had deteriorated. Despite his cheerleading, Avery's team was broken, and no one had acknowledged it. Unfortunately, positivity often gets a reality check well after suffering has accumulated.

This story presents us with the opportunity to discuss the Leader Effectiveness and the Management Team Coherence conversations. I call these the Together Conversations because, since "we are all in this together," asking for help from one another other is key. This story highlights the inevitability that each good leader (Avery, Don, and Burton) will encounter personal limits throughout their entire leadership journey. It also illustrates that every member of the management team needs to know how to accept and grow through personal limits: by asking for help, allowing others to care for you, and giving teammates permission to help you see blind spots.

Don had ready access to good data (eNPS) but did not know how to help the management team apply it. Burton wasn't connected well enough with Avery to address the issue directly. And Avery didn't know how to collaborate with his team, so he unknowingly solicited "dirty yeses," which result whenever a leader is committed to getting yes from his team. The short-term payoff is compliance, but dirty yeses cut off learning and collaboration and break the bond of connection between team members and their leader.

The management team's patterns were preventing the company from scaling, and they would continue to work the same coil in the Spiral of Growth until their ability to hold their conversational space matured. What does that repetition feel like? Imagine a mule hitched to a grindstone, circling round and round on the same path.

They did not have a process to help each leader address his or her effectiveness, and their coherence was limited by their conversational know-how and experience. Like so many management teams, they remained blind because of their patterns or lack of training. This is, unfortunately, the default.

The Employee Net Promoter Score

An eNPS is based on a one-question employee survey asking: "On a scale of 0 to 10, how likely are you to recommend (your company) to friends and family as a place to work?" By limiting this to one (and only one) question, two things happen: first, you get a quick, visceral reaction, and second, you get a high employee-response rate. At first glance, this score indicates the level of employee equity a leader has accrued, but it is also the best way I've found to assess employee engagement.

The calculation is as follows:

Those who respond with a 9–10 are promoters and correlate with "engaged."
Those who respond with a 7–8 are passives and correlate with "disengaged."
Those who respond with a 0–6 are detractors and correlate with "actively disengaged."

Subtracting the percentage of detractors from the percentage of promoters (ignoring the passives) generates Net Promoter Score. A score of fifty is considered good.

Since 2012, I have collected eNPS trend information on several companies with scores ranging from negative seven to eighty-one and, over time, I have watched how revenue and profit growth correlate. The eNPS is a leading indicator of sustainability and scalability.

Even though Avery's star had been rising due to high levels of profit growth, a low eNPS meant that most of Avery's employees were passively or actively disengaged. We could say that Avery's effectiveness as a leader was marginal and deteriorating, yet we still hadn't identified the root cause.

Before we move on, I'd like to invite you to once again step onto your personal viewing platform. Imagine yourself as Avery's CEO. What feelings and urges are present? Do you feel conflicted between the desire for growing profits and a need for long-term sustainability? How do you feel about his team's resistance? Now imagine yourself talking with Avery about this. As you anticipate a conversation, what feelings are you experiencing? How do you imagine Avery responding?

USING THE SCORES FOR YOUR BENEFIT

To define a root cause, you have to shift your mindset. I know Avery personally, and I know he wanted to experience personal growth. I was certain, given the right environment, he would pursue transformation with his whole heart, mind, and soul, and all his strength, but he would need a much clearer framework from which he and the entire leadership team could practice.

The first conversation, the Value Creation Conversation, introduces a fresh mindset—a framework as the basis for the conversation. If you diligently do the work required by this framework and continually keep this conversation in awareness, you establish a solid foundation for the subsequent conversations. (However, this conversation alone will not ensure sustainability).

Next, the Execution Conversation is the place where you define the tactics that will deliver the Value Creation formula. In addition to tactics, your staff's "willingness and ability" to produce is critical. Now the nature of the conversations begin to shift from strategic through tactical and then to relational.

I find that many leaders have an ability to focus on only one of the three types—if they are strategic, they are often limited tactically or relationally; if they are relational, they might be limited strategically or tactically. As we move further into our conversations, the relational aspect of leadership becomes more prominent. It must be cultivated and maintained within the tension of strategy and tactics. Our conversations and their metrics are designed to sustain this tension.

I'd like to invite you to explore a mindset shift through the metaphor of a garden. Before we began construction on our home, my wife and I invested in a good landscape architect. We walked the land together while reviewing the blueprints of the house, and the architect asked questions and offered suggestions that led to the beautiful garden that surrounds our home today. But it needs to be tended regularly; without continual attention, it wouldn't be sustainable. With care, it continues to offer its beauty, and we continue to be inspired.

I liken a company, which is a community of people trying to create value for themselves and others, to a garden. When I walk among the plants and shrubs of my garden, I often notice dead branches that draw energy from the main part of the plant, so I prune them. This helps the plant flourish. The plant remains strong if the gardener tends and befriends it.

Avery's pattern of manipulating his team drew valuable energy away from sustainability and value creation because no one was tending the garden. Your management team is like a garden; unless it is designed for beauty and sustainability and tended well, it will deteriorate.

The management team behaviors within the Leader Effectiveness Conversations also need tending. The root cause of the issue we have been discussing involves architecture and tending. If the management team and leader effectiveness architecture had been playfully practiced by all members of the team and tended by Don and the other management team members, Avery's deteriorating eNPS would have been addressed long ago as an issue to process with the management team through Avery's own initiative. This step toward vulnerability and demonstration of courage would have further strengthened trust between members. Instead, I imagine, the glistening lure of increasing profits diverted energy away from tending.

Glorifying short-term sparkle is a powerful temptation. This behavior is a branch that needs pruning. Just as a lawn can be made greener by pouring on the fertilizer, profits can be made to grow by manipulation of various factors. But both have long-term costs to sustainability.

Avery may not have known how to increase his eNPS, but by asking for help and comparing his scores to those of his teammates, which were better, the path to learning would open. Certainly, his teammates would have asked him questions and helped him see his blind spots, and from this he would develop actionable insight.

When attended to properly, issue identification, processing, and aging usually provide the on-ramp into these Togetherness Conversations. When Don and I initially discussed his concern about Avery, I asked how they processed issues within the management team. He was honest and said, "Not very well." Further, we discovered that they didn't have a standard processing template and unresolved issues were not tracked and aged. It was clear that Don needed architecture; he wanted to become much better at tending and befriending. Growth in his own level of effectiveness was in order, and he was willing and able. By tending his garden, collaboration would flourish.

The Leader Effectiveness Conversation

Our brains and bodies have the innate capacity to both give and receive care; it's part of our genetic inheritance. Not only does survival depend on the fight or flight instinct, it also depends on the "tend and befriend' instinct. All mammals are born with an "attachment system"—a set of behaviors that allow for strong emotional bonds between caregivers and their young. The emotion of care comes naturally to us because our species would not be able to survive without it. The capacity to feel affection and interconnection is part of our biological nature. Our brains are designed to care.[9]

   With this understanding, we can begin to unpack the dynamic between Avery, Don, and Burton through the following conversational model. Let's begin by trying to understand the circle within the triangle.

Leader Effectiveness Conversation

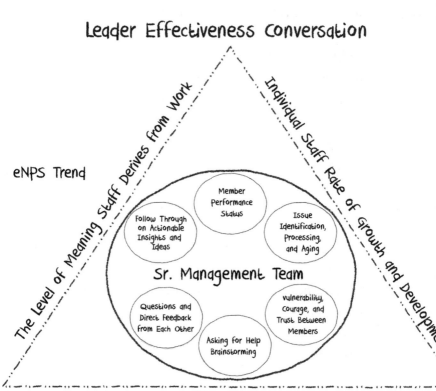

eNPS Trend

The Level of Meaning Staff Derives from Work

Individual Staff Rate of Growth and Development

Member Performance Status

Follow Through on Actionable Insights and Ideas

Issue Identification, Processing, and Aging

Sr. Management Team

Questions and Direct Feedback from Each Other

vulnerability, courage, and Trust Between Members

Asking for Help Brainstorming

Staff Contribution

A management team moves their company forward by creating initiatives that build on or mitigate company strengths, weaknesses, opportunities, and threats. Keeping each other posted on progress is critical because it's normal to encounter unforeseen obstacles. These obstacles are described as *issues*. When *caring* is present, the management team can help resolve issues; but, in the absence of caring, unresolved issues can become a sign of weakness and the team avoids them. Without vulnerability, a management team cannot be effective; but, with vulnerability, each member can ask for help, receive it, and feel empowered and more connected. The circle within our model describes the behavior expected of the management team members during their weekly meeting.

Don's company intended for companywide eNPS to progressively improve from quarter to quarter throughout the year. To them, eNPS was a leading indicator of employee engagement, which was a weakness they needed to overcome. While they had collected eNPS data on each business unit, the management team container hadn't yet become a place for each member's performance to be safely reviewed. You can see where this is headed; it's called pairing.

Pairing results when the authority figure (Don) isn't sponsoring tension-filled conversations within the management team container. In this case, Burton surfaced an issue with Don on a person-to-person basis instead of processing it at their weekly ninety-minute management team meeting. This "issue" started as an execution-related one because Avery's staff was unresponsive–their "willingness or ability" to produce was the "presenting" problem. When leaders unknowingly manipulate staff by urging them to comply without objection, they eliminate a space for "no" or "what if," and now they have become objects for manipulation. We all know how this ends.

At this point, the senior management team pattern between Avery, his team, Burton, and Don was diverting energy into waste. The unproductive way this issue emerged was not that unusual as these were deeply embedded patterns, and they set Don up as a traffic cop.

Optimally, Avery would have confronted his blind spot if his peers on the management team had been prepared, but they weren't. The responsibility for this would be Don's until he made it clear how the management team operates.

Within the structure of our Leadership Effectiveness Conversation, "staff contribution" forms the important foundation. In Avery's case, staff contribution had seriously deteriorated because the "level and quality of meaning staff derives from work" had plummeted. This tends to always be the case when leaders convert staff from meaning-seeking contributors to objects for manipulation, as Avery unknowingly had. The long-term cost to the business is that "staff rate of growth and development"—a key requirement for scaling and sustainability—erodes. If this corrosive pattern is sustained, a leadership reset will eventually be required, and years of confusion will most likely surround this event.

The Management Team Conversation

Your senior management team is a container that holds the real and the ideal in connection with each other through conversation. This is the place where the conversations invite us to encounter ourselves, reality, and our dreams together. Each time we meet, a threshold presents itself, and to cross this threshold, greater levels of courage and vulnerability must be found within. Your management team can become an exhilarating place of order and coherence from which robust value creation can increasingly flow.

As we see in the Leader Effectiveness Conversation diagram, the management team behaviors exist within that larger conversation. While they are very interdependent, it is helpful to maintain a structure for each. Maintaining the Leader Effectiveness Conversation is the responsibility of each management team member. If their willingness and ability to cross this threshold deteriorates, the management team deteriorates. Separating structure allows two things to occur within our management team:

1. As each conversational structure is designed as a playful practice field, you can begin each management team meeting with a review of this structure. Then, you can initiate your check-in by asking each member to share an assessment regarding their "effectiveness" since your last meeting.

2. At the conclusion of each meeting, you can have the group assess how effective their senior management team conversation was. Do this by giving time for each member to write down a list of behaviors to stop, start, and continue. Have each member share this.

When these assessments happen within your management team conversation, your leaders will find a deeper inner awareness and fluency that empowers them to be more effective.

Togetherness through the Inner Journey
I want to take you back to the study done by the University of Washington research team that I mentioned in the Introduction. In their report, they stated that the level of trust had dramatically

grown and because of this, organic collaboration (engagement) had emerged throughout the region. This created unusual growth and profitability.

They attributed the improved trust to the practices we deployed through the monthly management team meetings. What they didn't mention was that vulnerability had become a core behavior. Each member of the management team had discovered within their interior life a dormant capacity to accept themselves and their personal limitations in the presence of peers. When they practiced this, it gave their peers a chance to care. In fact, as their experiences with this accumulated, they each noticed an emerging creative inner resilience, and their limitations became just another part of being human. They were much more fun to be with—they seemed free.

In other words, their inner journey together helped them accept all parts of themselves without shame. Their connection as humans formed the foundation for their work together. This is called wholeness or wellness and it sponsors coherence.

When a management team has no need to hide from limitations, all things seem to magically work together, and this is how management team coherence forms. A management team needs space to practice, a space where an impasse is transformed by play. Remember, the management team is the epicenter of your enterprise, and whatever happens within it ripples and quakes into every person within your company.

Coherence grows as individual and team awareness grow. As management teams become more aware of themselves and others through these conversations, they increasingly upgrade the quality of their connection, collaboration, and work.

As we continue exploring these conversations, please keep in mind that even though the Execution Conversation is where most of your employees will logically be directed to focus their energy, Leader Effectiveness and Management Team Coherence are vital to the success of Execution. Why?

Execution requires the willingness and ability of your important people—their engagement. To be engaged, they must feel like they can and want to do the work. But, we know from the Gallup workforce study about engagement that, in the typical company, two thirds of employees are not engaged. What's going on?

Take a moment to review the following snapshot from the 2016 Government Census on Business (the most recent as of this writing)[10]

Enterprise Employment Size	20-499
Establishment Births 2015-2016	50,756
Change in Employment	1,477,514
Establishment Deaths 2015-2016	44,183
Change in Employment	1,355,436
Establishment Expansions 2015-2016	407,898
Change in Employment	3,160,269
Establishment Contractions 2015-2016	367,321
Change in Employment	2,711,350

When an employee unwillingly departs a company, their ability to trust again is also impaired. More than four million employees bring a cautiousness into their next place of employment. And, this is happening every year!

Not only are we losing talent, but the psyche of our national workforce is being harmed, making it more and more difficult to cultivate engagement. The cumulative impact to our society is staggering. Achieving sustainability is a vital priority. Many companies are stuck in a doom loop—a closed coil. No wonder engagement is so low. Leader Effectiveness and Management Team Coherence conversations start with caring!

CHAPTER 5
THE COLLABORATION CONVERSATION

Jenifer was introduced to me by a member of my Vistage CEO group as the future leader of a sizable second-generation family company. In one of my initial meetings with her and the company's hired-gun CEO, I asked, "What's the purpose of your company?" They responded automatically, "To increase the family's wealth."

As I let this answer land on me, I *sensed* flat energy. Nothing between them seemed to resonate. These words were like placeholders occupying a safe and politically correct spot in their script. They offered words with no expression.

If it's true that the purpose we serve generates the questions we collaborate around, I wondered how their management team collaborated around "increasing the family's wealth." I thought that if the management team was all family, these words might indeed create traction. So, during our next meeting, I decided to find out.

Jenifer shared that they didn't tell managers about their purpose because it would be awkward. Instead, they set goals for their managers to achieve. While this way of structuring a business wasn't foreign to me, I did wonder how well it was working, so I asked, "How frequently do the managers achieve the goals you set?"

Jenifer paused. She shifted her eyes, her cheeks flushed, and she said, "Well, that's part of the problem. They don't achieve them often enough." The problem was that the goals they were setting were placeholders, too.

Since goals are meant to be a steering mechanism for collaboration, and purpose is the basis for a company's existence, it was no wonder they weren't achieving goals. Unless everyone finds meaning and energy through movement toward purpose, collaboration will always be weak.

Even though impasses were accumulating, Jenifer and the CEO held onto their stated purpose . . . at least when they were together. When owners deem that their interests supersede the interests of those who create value, there is no sustainable basis for collaboration. When everyone pursues their own best interests while giving the impression that they are on board with something else, sustaining a lie becomes the basis for working together.

Eventually, Jenifer shared that she wasn't satisfied and that she wanted to either create something special or move outside the family business. But, in the early season of our collaboration, she didn't have a space to explore what was going on within her, and therefore she couldn't access her heart. So, she continued to use MBA-oriented language, talking about wanting faster growth, better execution, more effective leaders, and a dramatic shift in the products and services they offered.

Questions are the driveshaft of collaboration

Many of our early conversations focused on her desire to diversify the company into technology through acquisition, and she wanted me to collaborate with her on how she could do this. But no potent questions were available, so collaboration was simply a red herring and a time waste.

Are you seeing the pattern? By primarily concentrating on the outward desires of growth, value creation, and execution, Jenifer avoided what was going on "within" her. Just as we all frequently do, she unconsciously chose to stay where she felt most comfortable—in the space of her MBA persona, focusing her mind and words on tactics and strategy and away from her feelings. This invisible pattern was blocking her ability to lead.

Questions are the driveshaft of collaboration, so, if Jenifer were going to create something special, the questions would need to change. To start, Jenifer needed to see and accept herself

Your primary work as a leader is to become deeply "aware."

as she really was—a flawed human learning her way into effective leadership, just like all of us. Without this vulnerability, the flow of potential for her company would remain constrained and collaboration would feel managed.

The Inward and Outward Work of Collaboration

As we continue to explore these conversations, it's best to think of collaboration as the "activity" that is "value creation." Collaboration is where the tangible and intangible come together. It's where the interior movements within each person set the tone—the powerful inner currents that push their way into the visible: a smile, a frown, words, silence, fight, flight, freeze, or appease. The outward behaviors and actions that drive results originate invisibly within and between us.

Dear friend, if I could sum up the message of this book in only one word, I would say your primary work as a leader is to become deeply "aware." Without this, you cannot sponsor robust collaboration. It is from this solid inner stance that organic collaboration can flow. Collaboration is value creation.

Whether intentional or not, collaboration, in general, always has a facilitator or sponsor, and this person is also the "tone setter." The tone you set creates the feeling or mood you expect. Most collaborations do not start with conscious tone-setting. Instead, they start with the frenetic energy of urgency, which unconsciously sets the tone. Because of this, they never achieve the possible. Tension combined with frenetic energy destroys value and creates waste.

THE TENSION OF DIVERGENCE

Eminent economist E.F. Schumacher, in his classic book *Small Is Beautiful: A Study of Economics as If People Mattered*, describes the life most people live as one of trying to reconcile opposites, which cannot, by definition, be reconciled. He describes convergent problems as those that can be solved by logical reasoning, and divergent problems as those to which logic cannot be applied effectively. He goes on to say:

> When [convergent problems] have been solved, the solution can be written down and passed on to others, who can apply it without needing to reproduce the mental effort necessary to find it. Divergent problems, as it were, force man to strain himself to a level above himself; they demand, and thus provoke the supply of forces from a higher level, thus bringing love, beauty, goodness, and truth into our lives. It is only with the help of these higher forces that opposites can be reconciled in the living situation. To have to grapple with divergent problems tends to be exhausting, worrying and wearisome. Hence people try to avoid it and to run away from it. [11]

Schumacher can help us understand why it is so diffi-cult for each of us to be present with reality and help others be there, too, and why most leaders are not equipped to stay with the tension that arises out of divergent problems, and allow that tension to do its work. Yet being present is exactly what I believe is necessary.

Before I go much further, it's important to explain that most of the problems I encounter that make it so difficult to estab-lish sustainable companies are divergent problems. Yet it's my observation that leaders naturally prefer to spend their time on *convergent problems—the kind that have been solved by hundreds and thousands of companies, time and time again.* Books, speak-ers, workshops, and most consultants and coaches create value by sharing these solutions. With so much support for convergent problems already documented, why do they seem to occupy almost all of our time?

Staying in the tension of unresolved divergent problems for a long time is exhausting, especially when your "perceiver" is broken. Perceiving requires time and distance, while analysis takes a microscopic view. Perceiving brings about a mindset shift, while analysis brings more information. When all you have is your current, limited toolbox of ideas—what you've learned based on your experience—you are bound to

The quality of our collaboration forms the outcome.

eventually encounter the closed circle of a doom loop. You need to upgrade the toolbox of ideas that guide how you perceive the world.

Let's take a deeper look at the well-established ideas of quantum physics, entanglement, and neuroscience, which suggest that the flow of energy and information to us, within us, and between us is raw potential. It only takes form when observed. This idea also tracks with what the wisdom traditions of many major religions have shared for centuries —we are co-creators!

Now consider the implications. *How we hold our attention, within and between us, determines what we create together.* In other words, the quality of our collaboration forms the outcome.

Attempting to collaborate through the plateau or descent part of the growth cycle while being in an interior state of rigidity or chaos will only reinforce the patterns of the past. It is critical to allow the tension to not only help wake you up to your patterns but to break through them as well. Let the tension do its work in and between you and your team.

Doing the Work of Collaboration

Each of our conversations is a "collaboration generator." When you create a clearly defined conversational framework, you will encourage quality questions. Potent questions always sponsor tension, and when we stay in the conversation, tension will do its work. The following illustration will guide our discussion of working in collaboration.

To help you understand tone-setting, start by reviewing the first column: Mood, Theme, The Meaning of Work, and Customer. The second column—"Me"—in my experience, represents about twenty percent of the workforce, and they are *actively* disengaged. Since they withdraw from tension, what tone do you imagine they bring to a collaboration? The next column, "Me and Them," represents about fifty percent–they are much more common. The tone they bring is certainly an upgrade, but their capacity to allow the tension to do its work is still extremely limited. They stuff the tension, and by doing this, they limit the potency of questions.

The Collaboration Conversation

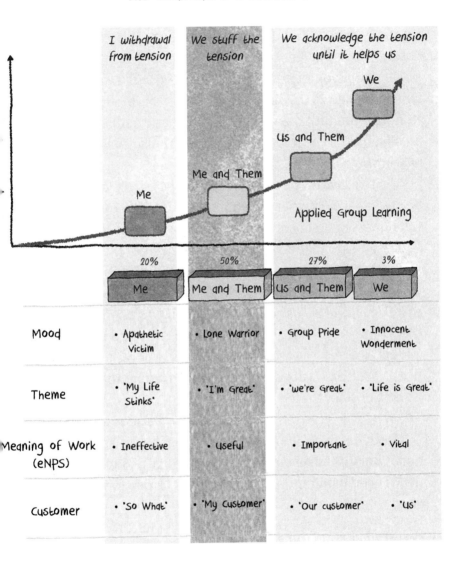

	Me	Me and Them	Us and Them	We
	20%	50%	27%	3%
Mood	• Apathetic Victim	• Lone Warrior	• Group Pride	• Innocent Wonderment
Theme	• 'My Life Stinks'	• 'I'm Great'	• 'We're Great'	• 'Life is Great'
Meaning of Work (eNPS)	• Ineffective	• Useful	• Important	• Vital
Customer	• 'So What'	• 'My Customer'	• 'Our customer'	• 'Us'

These two columns force most companies to micromanage collaboration.

As we shift into the third column that includes "Us and Them" and "We," we begin to see that the tone improves and the capacity to name the tension expands. This is where organic collaboration thrives.

Once you get the hang of working with the conversations (which are each a collaboration) through this model, you will start to notice the attitude and intention that each person brings to a collaboration. You will also learn to notice these same things within yourself.

While attitude and intention are invisible, they are the tie-rods that hold your collaboration together. They indicate the willingness or ability of each person to sponsor flow.

In the highest state, where maybe three percent of management teams operate, "wonderment" seems to describe a childlike expectation of being awakened to something like *grace*, by which I mean to be surprised by insights that come from beyond us.

Tension turns to stress whenever we start to feel separate from each other.

Why do I place such a priority on letting the tension do its work? Consider these three realities:

First, we can readily sense tension through all eight senses. Our body-brain nervous system is wired to sense things like this, but bringing it into awareness is an upgrade. Authentic collaboration is filled with tension, so it's a perfect place to practice awareness!

Second, if we don't bring tension into awareness, it will separate us, which is why collaboration then becomes managed. If you want organic collaboration, name the tension!

Third, tension turns to stress whenever we start to feel

separate from each other—this usually means that you are at risk of a loss of connection. When we name the tension, the sense of separation dissipates, and openness begins to manifest. Therefore tone-setting by way of naming the tension is vital.

Last, tension and anxiety always accompany potent questions. If these aren't present, you aren't focused on the right question.

Think of it this way: if you and another person each hold one end of a very large rubber band and slowly stretch it toward its maximum capacity, both tension and anxiety are present. If either of you react to anxiety and release the tension, connection is broken, and trust is broken. Alternatively, you could talk about the tension and the anxiety and the temptation to withdraw or react, and then decide together what to do. A collaboration around a potent question can feel this way. I sometimes bring a very large rubber band into these meetings as a symbol of our practice. While attitude, mood, and intention are invisible, the experience they sponsor is tangible. Experiences like these make collaboration meaningful.

David Brooks published an opinion piece in the *New York Times* that I believe can shed light on how collaboration can work. Brooks said, "...[A] defining question for any school or company is: What is the quality of the emotional relationships here? ... Do you have a metric for measuring relationship quality? Do you have teams reviewing relationship quality? Do you know where relationships are good and where they are bad?" [12]

Putting relationship quality at the core is the basis for organic collaboration.

MAKING THE TURN

As we move further into collaboration, try to place yourself in this next story by once again moving to your personal viewing platform. Ask yourself with which person or stance you most identify.

Steve, the company owner and CEO, started this management team collaboration with the Growth Conversation by sharing (with lots of words) his strong commitment to rapidly grow the company. His tone was one of conviction. When Ann Marie, the CFO, thoughtfully responded that she didn't think the execution part of the company was on firm enough ground, they became stuck.

Steve's energy seemed rigid. He stuffed the tension, leaned in toward the table, and began telling her about growth. With this, Ann Marie moved a couple of inches back, and the opportunity to hear from her was lost. At the same time, Joe, the leader who owned execution, stuffed the tension by filling the space with talking without saying much for a while. Can you see the tension working in this story? Their relationship was tenuous.

At this point, I asked them to pause and notice the energy they were feeling and to point to where they each were on the collaboration illustration. After a bit, Steve said, "I'm reacting;" Ann Marie said, "I'm withdrawing;" and Joe said, "I'm also reacting." We went on to discuss what was happening, and then Steve said to Ann Marie, "I hadn't ever heard your concern about execution before. Maybe you've been trying to tell me, but I wasn't willing to listen. I'm sorry."

Side-tracking starts just like this. Many collaborations end with one person thinking all is well while the others feel disconnected. Paying attention to the energy and naming it can be helpful for identifying where collaboration is breaking down.

While the Growth Conversation was the launching point, Ann Marie offered a potent question around execution, which is where elevated tension was felt by all. In their desire for more growth, many CEOs/owners don't want to hear that execution needs work, so they short-circuit the collaboration. This means the tension sent them into reaction or withdrawal. Steve, Ann Marie, and Joe needed to have an intentional conversation about collaboration in order to recover their broken connection. Reviewing the conversational model makes admitting mistakes more possible, and this encourages humility.

I hope you are starting to see how each conversation relates to all the others. You must have solid ground in the other conversations before you can really scale growth. If I hadn't asked them to name where they were on the collaboration curve, a window of opportunity would have closed. I call this "the turn." Turning toward yourself, seeing the habituated energy that you just contributed—which created waste—and sharing in humility is the first and most difficult step toward creating solid inner ground. Bringing the parts of yourself that have been in hiding into the light is exceptionally powerful.

As you continue to work with the conversations and the collaboration illustration, your capacity for live-action coaching can also improve. When you sense that you or someone else is withdrawing or reacting to the tension, you might gently bring this to their attention and ask, "How can I help you shift?" By approaching every collaborative experience as playful practice, the entire team will, imperfectly but with humor, travel the performance curve of our model together and become more sustainable.

Exhaustion and impasse can go hand in hand, but by shifting your toolbox of ideas, you can open a door to new thresholds of perception.

Crossing the Threshold to Inner Fluency

Jenifer initially wanted to apply the toolbox of ideas she acquired through her MBA program. She tried for quite a while. Eventually, though, as we allowed the tension to do its work, our collaboration started to address what was going on *within* her. As we shifted away from the impotent conversations associated with her MBA mindset, we approached an unfamiliar threshold and the questions became more potent.

Our collaborations now started with, "What are you frustrated with?," and "What has happened that has you feeling that way?" Jenifer began to accept that her stuck feelings were generating powerful emotional currents that were becoming harder and harder to stuff. We'll talk more about this in the Inner-Fluency Conversation, but her state of being became more rigid and her leadership less potent. Jenifer finally came to the point of accepting these things about herself. The tension helped her embrace humility. This was how her "turn" happened.

As we continued to collaborate, Jenifer admitted that she tolerated falling short of goals because she doubted that she was competent enough to attract and lead more capable leaders. When she uttered, "What do *I* have to give them?," I knew we were finally ready to exit the doom loop. This vulnerable question seemed to underpin the way Jenifer acted, so allowing it to come to the surface and then sitting with it in silence was necessary.

The following illustration of the doom loop demonstrates what keeps us trapped in a comfortable but unhealthy pattern and what it takes to break free from it and move into a new pattern that leads to growth. At the center of every doom loop is an unresolved issue, and most often, this is a divergent problem.

Strengthening the Inside Edge

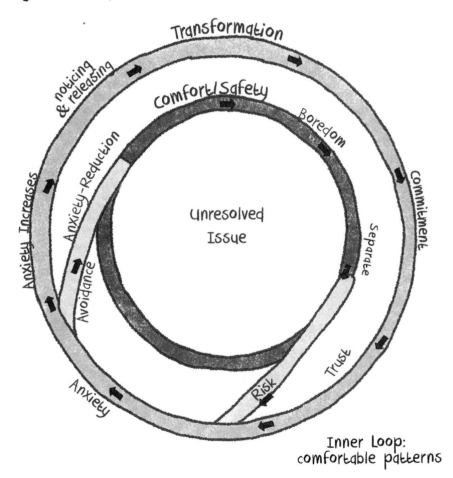

Outer Loop:
...ding with new patterns

Transformation

noticing & releasing

Comfort/Safety

Boredom

Anxiety-Reduction

Anxiety Increases

Commitment

Avoidance

Separate

Unresolved Issue

Anxiety

Trust

Risk

Inner Loop:
comfortable patterns

ENTERING THE SPACE OF SILENCE

Over the years, I've noticed that silence and wise leadership seem to go hand in hand. When Jenifer vulnerably ventured, "What do I have to give them?," a part of me, my personality, wanted to relieve the tension by providing an answer; but, a much deeper "me" knew that holding the silence would accomplish more. If I answered, I would cut off all possibility of being surprised.

Silence isn't the absence of noise or sound; it's the presence of reality. Everything you see, hear, feel, or sense emanates from silence. Unfortunately, we are uncomfortable in silence because it doesn't map with the frenetic, ruminating, fitful flow of energy that we have become so addicted to.

Silence is the place where an infinite number of possibilities exists.

Robert Sardello is co-director of the School of Spiritual Psychology. He is a faculty member of the Dallas Institute of Humanities and Culture and a former chairman of the Department of Psychology, University of Dallas. He talks about the role of silence in relationship to the soul:

> The word resonance comes from the Latin word *resonare*, meaning, "return to sound." When we sound an object such as a bell, it continues to ring or resonate the original sound. There is another kind of resonance called sympathetic resonance: when a bell sounds and continues to resonate, another object with qualities of the same pitch as the bell begin to vibrate with it. The human soul functions similarly as an activity of resonance, and our soul connection with Silence is a form of sympathetic resonance.[13]

Silence is the backdrop for all organic collaboration. Cultivating a capacity to be in silence and resonate with its feel allows us to become present to possibility. Think back to a time when you were in a meeting discussing a problem and the tension became noticeable. As the tension increased, how did your peers behave? Typically, when I ask that question, I'm told that they couldn't hold the tension or the silence. When we speak or act from a place of anxiety, we eliminate the possible; but, when we allow the tension to do its work, we are cultivating an innate capacity to be with silence. Silence is the place where an infinite number of possibilities exists.

The poet Kabir said:

Be silent in your mind, silent in your senses,
And also, silent in your body.
Then, when all these are silent, don't do anything.
In that state, truth will reveal itself to you.
It will appear in front of you and ask,
"What do you want?"[14]

Within the realm of silence, "feeling knowing" becomes evident. Our body-brain nervous system resonates with the subtle energy of truth. This "feeling knowing" allows us to sense our ability to transcend divergent problems and our historical invisible patterns. Who we are becomes larger and more capable of accepting wisdom as a gift.

As Jenifer offered her question and allowed silence to remain, intimacy emerged. Giving voice to her inner doubts and allowing silence to hold what she had shared created an open space within her cluttered psyche. Silence allowed Jenifer to accept herself as she was and start to move on.

Within us is a still point that nothing can disturb. This is our center, a place where destiny draws us forward, if we, too, can be still. The question "What do I have to give them?" comes from a place of personality. When we only experience personality, we naturally hide what we believe is a shortcoming. But when we repeatedly touch the place of silence within by practicing, we taste a presence that draws us to itself. We experience something like being held. Here, our "felt sense" knows that all is well. As Jenifer let silence do its work, a limiting belief came to the surface. She believed she was inadequate as a leader and that others were more capable. The MBA language was simply a mask to hide it.

Intimacy with our center is a rare experience in today's culture. While cultivating this capacity is vital, always remaining in your center isn't possible. Wholeness is, though. What is wholeness? Wholeness comes from a willingness to explore the inexhaustible, multifaceted dimensions of ourselves—not just the parts that embarrass us or bring us shame or guilt, or the armor with which we suit up to protect ourselves; it also includes our gifts, capabilities, and capacities. As we become more whole, others will experience the courage to also embrace wholeness. This is when a management team reaches coherence and when organic collaboration really takes off. This is why the practices in the *work* section are so valuable.

Over time I noticed that, as Jenifer's experience of wholeness grew, her capacity for patience developed. With this, divergent problems, the impasses that require us to transform, began to dissolve. What she had previously been powerless to overcome became immaterial. Jenifer was transcending those issues.

Finding Solid Ground

Organic collaboration requires solid ground within and between each member of the management team. Solid ground is strengthened when:

- the reason we exist together creates meaning, and what happens to one, happens to all;
- an intense sense of interpersonal connection is maintained through humility;
- facing and helping others see reality (mutual risk-taking) is the norm; and,
- we converse truthfully about our individual and joint performance.

When any of these deteriorate, the ground becomes wobbly.

As Vistage speaker Pat Murray reminds me, the ground can also become very wobbly when the authority figure unconsciously acts to remove the tension or anxiety around the questions on which the team needs to collaborate.

When Jenifer became the president, she shared that while she was excited about the progress she'd made, she also carried a greater sense of responsibility. She felt a bit uncertain about how to move forward organizationally. She believed the company could benefit from more experienced sales and marketing leadership. To bring this into the team, she wanted to hire a COO or CMO from outside.

As we discussed her ideas, it became clear that while she hadn't brought this question to the management team, she had discussed it with the members individually. She went on to explain that in her individual conversations with each one, she had sensed posturing, so she'd decided to collect input and make the final decision on her own. Posturing means that wobbly ground is present, and Jenifer was about to circumvent the needed tension.

Let's revisit our conversational models. The conversations Jenifer was trying to sponsor were about *growth* and *value creation*.

Although she couldn't describe it as such, she had assumed that the *quality and quantity of customer* interactions and the *potency of their offerings* were subpar and that none of the current leadership team were capable of collaborating through this. And she also had unilaterally created a solution, which was to bring someone in from the outside. Jenifer was trying to avoid the tension and anxiety of collaborating with her team. Unknowingly, she was also transferring her own feelings of inadequacy onto her team.

I shared with her that I thought she was missing an opportunity to strengthen the ground. By creating a solution without team collaboration, Jenifer was inadvertently becoming the Messiah. She was relieving herself of the tension and anxiety that come with creating space for others to awkwardly work through an objective evaluation and recommendation process. By sponsoring a collaboration with the entire team around the specific dimensions of the Growth Conversation, with specific assignments, she would be reconnecting everyone with their new purpose, which was anchored in Employee and Customer Net Promoter Score data.

The impasse she was experiencing existed within her, and it was fear-based. Her desire to escape the tension would erode the new purpose the company was trying to serve, and while it might seem expedient, over the long haul, sustainability would deteriorate. Management team coherence can only be achieved when the most difficult collaborations create solid ground upon which the team can stand.

THE INNER STATE OF YOUR AUTHORITY

Collaboration and authority have an important and sometimes awkward relationship, and understanding this relationship can help you move toward organic collaboration. This is the point where it may be helpful for us to clarify how authority manifests itself.

Mr. Fields, the assistant principal at the high school I attended, held an elevated space on the organizational chart, and his title alone created authority. By being elevated to this high place, he acquired a platform, a place from which to act. The platform itself created no authority. It was his threatening presence that caused all of us to be wary around him. Mr. Fields used the force of his words and his demeanor to maintain control. However, he did not cultivate my growth and development, and I believe his platform was wasted. He was an authority figure, but he held no authority with me.

On the other hand, my sister-in-law Chris is also an assistant principal, and a big part of her role is to help kids and parents who are struggling to regain traction. The kids who come her way are sent by other teachers, sometimes over and over. She collaborates with these teachers, the students, and the parents toward a positive outcome. No matter what the challenge each child is facing, Chris always sets the tone by making sure they understand that nothing about them is broken, that everyone makes mistakes, and that she cares more about them than the mistake they have made. Chris has authority with students, parents, and teachers because she fosters meaningful collaboration in challenging

The less superficial a person is, the greater their authority.

situations. She sets the tone with her presence, and this creates an amazing opportunity for her to use her platform to fulfill her destiny. Her work is "vital to meaning."

Remember that each of the conversations is intended as a collaboration generator and each requires an owner. With this picture in mind, we can explore how the quality of authority drives the quality of collaboration.

David Brooks shared an experience while teaching at Yale:

> A few years ago, when I was teaching at Yale, I made an announcement to my class. I said that I was going to have to cancel office hours that day because I was dealing with some personal issues and a friend was coming up to help me sort through them. I was no more specific than that, but that evening 10 or 15 students emailed me to say they were thinking of me or praying for me. For the rest of the term the tenor of that seminar was different. We were closer. That one tiny whiff of vulnerability meant that I wasn't some aloof Professor Brooks, I was just another schmo trying to get through life.[15]

The less superficial a person is, the greater their authority. One can say that people have authority in proportion to what they unite within themselves—the *wholeness* that brings their interior parts together. This experience of authority is true and unique. All companies are a platform; so, abundant opportunities for collaboration and authority are apparent.

Every collaboration has an authority figure and, to the degree that the authority figure is consciously living from his or her center, or interior platform, he or she will not be pulled off track.

Now consider how the state of your interior platform (rigidity, chaos, or harmony) is unconsciously being transmitted to those around you, and how we "sense" what is going on within each other. Your inner state is *always* being transmitted to those you are collaborating with.

When authority figures use their organizational platform to tell, explain, and convince, how might you describe the state of their interior? What authority does their presence transmit? We all know that people like this use many words to feel secure and to calm their own anxiousness. They have no authority, but they do have a platform, and their attempts at collaboration will simply waste time and support low engagement.

Kurt Lewin was a German-American psychologist, known as one of the modern pioneers of social, organizational, and applied psychology in the United States. Lewin taught:

> All actions are based on the ground the person happens to stand on. The firmness of his actions, and the clearness of his decisions depend largely upon the stability of this ground, although he himself may not even be aware of its nature. What-ever a person does or wishes to do, he must have some ground to stand on. This is probably the primary reason why he is extremely affected the moment the ground on which he stands begins to give way. One of the most important constituents of the ground on which the individual stands is the "social group" to which he belongs.[16]

Back to our earlier idea: quantum physics, entanglement, and neuroscience are suggesting that the flow of energy and infor-mation to us, within us, and between us is raw potential that takes form when observed. Now consider the implications. What holds our attention, as well as when and how we hold our attention, within and between us, determines what we create together. In other words, the quality of the collaboration forms the outcome. If

Jenifer continued to unconsciously focus on eliminating her anxiety, the outcomes would simply strengthen the doom loop.

Divergent problems, like wobbly management team ground, are not solved; they can be transcended through quality collaboration and the awareness that unfolds from it. This is what happened for Jenifer. Allowing the company purpose to evolve into something larger and more inclusive of others created a tension that forced her to become more aware.

Leadership formation accelerates when impasses are acknowledged with humility in the presence of others who can help. The kind of collaboration that we've been discussing becomes more and more necessary.

Growing self-awareness can open you to an ocean of fresh possibilities that are waiting to be shaped by you, just as they were for Jenifer. And, the foundation of organic collaboration is connection.

CHAPTER 6
THE CONNECTION CONVERSATION

Bill, a member of Richard's management team (introduced in Chapter 2), habitually deflected the conversation onto another topic any time a Value Creation Conversation involved one of his initiatives. Sometimes, he did this with humor and sarcasm. Other times, he told a story (and the drama that it included) about how challenging it was to achieve what he was attempting to accomplish. Usually, this persuaded the other members of the management team to let the conversation slide.

Bill felt threatened because his connection to his center wasn't very stable, and the management team disconnected from Value Creation Conversations because they felt wobbly. Bill was a habitual side-tracker, but no one brought this to the table.

In my experience, being triggered into fight, flight, freeze, or appease is why so many leaders are unable to stay present to reality. With practice (the work), our capacity to be present grows quickly.

The quality of the way energy and information flow drives how I experience you, myself, and our future state, and how we work with that flow governs our willingness and ability to make wise choices. By growing in your ability to be present, you connect to yourself and to others. Access to wisdom grows within a connected group of leaders.

Attention is the process that directs the flow of energy and information being created between people as well as within people. Bill *sensed* the threat of losing his standing in Richard's management team, so his attention was hijacked, and that shifted energy to deflecting and protecting.

Connecting with *Now*

The conversations from this point forward are increasingly about *now*, and the previous conversations have primarily been oriented to *future* and *past*. If you linger with this a bit, you will quickly agree that *now* is all we really have. What I pay attention to *now* determines what I do now and who I do it with. How we hold *now* determines the future, and attention is the capacity to be with *now*. When our attention is distracted by anticipating the future—which is what Bill was doing—we separate from our center, and this fragmented presence loses contact with the subtle energy of potential that is always flowing. Connection is broken.

If energy and information flow as unformed potential, what shapes the form that energy takes or how it shows up in the future? The theory I've referenced throughout the book around entanglement is what points us to the answer: unformed potential becomes tangible as it is observed. That same flow of potential remains unformed until observation (attention) happens. Focusing on what we worry about makes our lives small and our company unsustainable. By doing the work to increasingly remain open, life enlarges, and the cycle of growth becomes invigorating. What captures our attention unfolds in our lives.

While scientists describe energy as unformed potential, spiritual traditions seem to each describe, in their unique vocabulary, the same thing, but all seem to embrace this presence as *grace*. While grace has hundreds of names, we all benefit from grace as our actions and intentions align *within* it.

Now, contrast this with a traditional mechanistic view of a company, which says that if each of the parts does its assigned job, the company will grow. I propose that this command-and-control view is one reason only thirty-three percent of employees are engaged; viewing people as parts cuts off the flow of grace.

Another view, one that is much more accurate and scientifically verifiable, is that each person in your company is part of a connected, luminous web, capable of sensing his or her way into self-organization and creativity when meaningfully connected. By helping everyone see themselves this way, the entire company begins to align naturally around its most noble purpose: the opportunity to create value. This self-organizing invisible field some call *grace* is wise beyond comprehension.

Pause now for just a few minutes and ask yourself these questions while making note of your answers:

- What has been my personal experience of the mystery of grace?
- Where is my attention now?
- What is the intention that wants to express itself through my life?

This fundamental interconnectedness that scientists call *entanglement* connects all things. While you can't measure entanglement or observe it through the five senses, it has been empirically established through decades of scientific research. Even though we can't see entanglement, our deep sensing knows how connected or disconnected we are.[17]

Take a moment now to think back to a time when you were not chosen to be on a team. Even today you can probably revisit the visceral experience associated with it. It's not an idea; it's a bodily sensation, an experience. Experience happens in relationship with others, and how we hold experience (the story we tell ourselves about it that has become encoded within us) shapes who we think we need to become.

When I left Vietnam as an intelligence analyst, the left mode of my brain was dominant for logical reasoning, looking for cause-and-effect relationships, and creating mental models. I told myself a story about who I was and how I would behave. As the descent part of my personal spiral of growth caused me to seek help, the right mode, which contextualizes the interconnectedness of things, became more pliable. This is where *relational meaning* is formed. Rather than perceiving specific, individual details, we *sense* their interrelatedness instead.[18]

As a leader, sensing the whole is more important than focusing on the parts. Right-mode perception sees between the lines, and left mode constructs lists, labels, and models. It decomposes the whole into parts for analysis.

The conversations we have tackled so far—the Outward-Moving Conversations, the Togetherness Conversations, and the Collaboration Conversation—are the conversations that create outward traction. They have been created through the left mode of the brain.

These conversations keep institutions moving forward. While the constraints within each conversation are conceptual, when activated within your team, they become conversational (between us and within us). The conversations activate the more holistic right mode of the brain. Then, tension—the very thing that's required to move us forward—becomes present. Staying connected to the conversations within and between us, while holding the tension, may be difficult initially; but, with practice,

Your patterns play out until your awareness kicks in.

the solid ground that reality demands emerges from within us, right where it has always been, from our very beginning. Staying in the tension requires a solid center, and living within the tension will strengthen our access to our center.

As we practice these conversations within the management team, the tension inevitably causes someone to wobble and thereby sidetrack the conversation. When a conversation becomes personal, it's natural to react by being defensive or withdrawing because we may sense a threat to our standing within our group. In other words, the inner state becomes contracted and we move into fight, flight, freeze, or appease. Your patterns play out until your awareness kicks in.

The Solid Ground of Connection

As we continue with Bill's story, we begin to understand why connection is so important. Because Bill had a strong connection with Richard, his CEO, and because Richard was modeling vulnerability during these meetings by acknowledging his own reactive patterns, Bill was cautiously and awkwardly willing to practice being present with the entire management team. Richard created the solid ground for Bill through their connection.

When Bill's habituated patterns tried to take the management team off-line, eventually, the other members began to demonstrate the courage and skill to successfully intervene. As their practice strengthened, Bill's support increased and the old patterns—the ones that caused him to sidetrack the conversation—were rewired by new experiences. Bill and the entire team were experiencing transformation by being in and maintaining tension and connection. They were crossing into the threshold of coherence.

Initially, Bill was more connected to wasteful patterns than to his management team; but, with practice, his need to separate and protect dissipated, and a natural connection emerged.

Bill's response is something each of us has experienced many times, and we know how off track we get because of it. This is a physical response to a perceived social threat.

Working the conversations with a playful attitude goes a long way toward minimizing the threat that one might lose their standing in the management team. And working together, playfully, can, over time, not only eliminate loss of connection but cause connection to become so strong that physical separation is transcended. And when this happens sidetracking disappears!

Over time, Bill was better able to stay connected to the conversation and his team members. Once that happened, the quality of his contribution increased. The management team can become a place of practice, and *there is no business problem that can't be solved when connection is strong.*

In descending through the Outward-Moving Conversations, we move more and more into an awareness of our interior. The Collaboration, Connection, Inner-Fluency, and Work Conversations then help us notice the flow of our interior life; and, as our connected lives become more flexible, adaptable, robust, and centered, members of the team help each other. The flow of energy and information in and between us grows qualitatively when a group's connection is cultivated in the following ways:

- attunement to our interior sense of ourselves (our felt sense of rigidity, chaos, and harmony—constriction and flow);
- attunement to the energy and information flow within the management team—is it flowing easily, or is there an elephant in the room?;

- attunement to the desired future state of the value creation community (company) and where we are now in the cycle of growth and our purpose;
- attunement to the limits, gifts, and contributions that each member brings, and bringing these to the attention of all.

This is how interactions within relationships shape attention interpersonally and guide attention internally. Practicing attunement within trusting relationships creates an increased tolerance to sit with emotions, images, bodily sensations, and behaviors that before may have felt too frightening or overwhelming to think about. As Bill practiced attunement, his center strengthened.

When a management team does the work, the social field of acceptance and receptivity becomes stronger. Members grow in their ability to remain centered and are less and less triggered by their fear response (fight, flight, freeze, and appease). This growth contributes to coherence. In this state, the team has gathered attention into a presence that feels more solid. This is how solid ground is developed, and we lead from inner solid ground.

SUSTAINABILITY FROM SOLID GROUND

Laura was an industry veteran with more than thirty years of experience. She had sold her own company to a larger public company and, from within that company, she continued to recruit and retain some of the best people in her industry.

When the 2008 downturn struck, the public company unloaded Laura's business unit to an even larger company. Within a year, that company also needed to go through a rapid downsizing. When it couldn't quickly find a buyer, it simply dissolved her business unit, sending hundreds of employees into the marketplace.

What happened over the next twenty-four months was unusual. While a few of the members of the management team kept me posted about their journey during this time, Laura called and we talked about the ideas that were forming within her. After the trauma she and her team had experienced from being divested twice, she wondered whether it would be possible for her to lead that group to another company or if they would choose to pursue individual paths.

To make a long story short, eighteen months later, 180 people came together again within another public company to become one of the fastest-growing entities within her industry. Five years later, despite severe systems and process limitations, there were 1,700 employees working from offices in several states, and the company was thriving. How was it possible to transcend these impasses?

In the preceding years, my work with Laura's management team had created a mysteriously strong bond of connection that rippled relationally over diverse geographical regions of the United States. While this connection was formed through the *work* they did together within an institution, it had become so strong and life-giving that an institution was no longer needed. When the team regrouped within the new company, they not only picked up where they left off, but who they had become through the impasse and struggle of the downturn transcended the original relationships. The energy and information flow—the team coherence—seemed to self-organize without a controlling institution.

Although the institutions that Laura had been associated with were no longer sustainable as platforms, the invisible solid ground of connection that had formed relationally between her team members continued to support the energy and information flow within and between them, beyond the institution. But these institutions served a very valuable purpose by providing a place of practice, where individual and relational transformation took place. Within these institutions, chemical markers were firmly established in the group's neuropathways through their shared meaningful experiences. Who they were together had become greater than who they had been.

Connection Is a Choice

At this point I'd like to invite you to enter the Connection Conversation with me through through the illustration that follows.

Connection is always a choice. Given this, it's important to understand that most people on the management team don't consciously think about their level of connection, so they have no choice about connecting yet. This graphic is designed to help you and your management team bring awareness to connection. By becoming aware of how we fit within the team, we can choose how we want to participate in learning and growth with our peers. As we increase our connection through the vulnerable dance of discovery, others can help us understand the "gift" we bring to the management team, and as we embrace our gift, we can give it more authentically. "Fit" happens when we and others are clear about ours gifts and how to use them. Coherence is strengthened when we express our intention regarding our fit. As coherence grows, the team can help us learn and adjust by bringing our blind spots into the light. This too can become organic.

FLOWING INTO CONNECTION

So, how did these 180 people on Laura's team stay connected? Their attention was attracted by the subtle energy of something larger and unseen. Their felt sense of entanglement was powerful.

The Connection Conversation

Upgrading our "fit" with each other—What is your intention?

How I apply learning	Level of "fit" I experince (gift)	Our connection to each other and beyond?
We help each other learn and adjust	"We are flourishing"	
I learn and adjust to help us	"My group is great"	
I learn and adjust to help me	"I'm great"	
I'm done learning and adjusting	"My life stinks"	

Inspired by the work of Dr. Dave Logan

Neuroscientist Dan Siegel described a gathering of a group of about 150 scientists, mostly physicists, on the topic of the connection of science and spirituality. In one of his workshops, he asked them to teach him what the term *spirituality* meant. To them, it meant being a part of something larger than a personal self, being connected to something greater, with a deeper meaning beyond the details of life, something beyond survival alone.[19]

Energy is the manifestation of potential flowing from infinite to finite, from uncertainty to certainty, from beyond us, into us, and between us.

The meaning Laura's team had created allowed them to transcend several divergent problems through connection.

When asked to define *energy*, the scientists explained it as something that manifests itself in different forms—light as protons, sound as airwaves, electricity as currents of electrical charges. But when asked what each of these forms has in common, the initial response from scientists was, "We don't know." When pushed, though, they'd say its potential. Potential to do stuff. In this view, energy is the manifestation of potential flowing from infinite to finite, from uncertainty to certainty, from beyond us, into us, and between us. It flows from potential to the realization of potential. It flows like a vast, unlimited river.

Laura's group manifested this sense of being connected to something larger and more meaningful than "self." While they were clearly attuned to the flow of potential, they were unable to articulate a description of what was drawing them to it. In other words, they were sensing their way into it—logic played no part.

But Connecting Is Physiological Too

Not long ago I traveled to Iowa for my fiftieth high school reunion. One afternoon, fifteen of us who had attended school together from kindergarten through grade twelve gathered at a classmate's home for a few hours. The conversations were amazing. We sat around in a circle and, one by one, stories emerged that transported us to a time more than sixty years ago, when our identities were formed through our connections. This is where a sense of "who I am" initially took root. The energy and information that had flowed through us all those years ago had produced chemical markers in our neuropathways, and these were automatically reactivated. Even though the connections had been dormant, they still existed.

Biologically speaking, every time you engage a <u>memory,</u> you *re-experience* it. The neurons that encode that memory are all firing the same way they did when the memory formed. This also means that you have an opportunity to <u>revise the memory</u> every time you recall it: with the original neurons firing, they're susceptible to making new connections or strengthening old ones. In other words, we can all grow. We are not captive to automatic behavior.

Through connection and the subjective way we experience ourselves, we form the identity we choose to try on. Our sense of ourselves emerges in the space between us when a bond of connection has formed or broken down. Strong connection is the firm ground that supports transformation and risk-taking. Being and becoming (transformation) need strong connection. Without this, we languish in separation. We all know this because deep down, we long to belong.

We can all grow. We are not captive to automatic behavior.

I now see that for many years, I was unconsciously connected to what I thought I needed to achieve to become who I thought I needed to be. I created plans about how I was going to make life better, but pain still managed to show up. By connecting primarily to my rational mind—the intellect—I tried to rise to the top of the culture that surrounded me, but I now see that only part of me was alive. By being primarily rational, I missed the flow of grace and wisdom and, with them, a deep, enduring sense of purpose. Purpose flows through the heart, while strategic plans are formulated rationally. Both are important, but one without the other is problematic.

Classic business leadership might say that passion, drama, intensity, and compelling emotion are qualities that are associated with the heart, and it might also say that these are desired states. As psychology has plumbed the depths of our psyche, a more current view of these qualities would say that these are indicators of agitation, and they are roadblocks to wise leadership and followership.

We often seek to overcome patterns that sidetrack us in order to find more stable ground and the corresponding peace of mind that we find there—to be liberated from reacting to circumstances. This can guide us into a new way of living and leading.

When our afflicted emotions are bottled up within us, the flow of creativity dries up. Survival thrives in this dark, damp, clammy place of rumination, and the channel of resourcefulness becomes a small trickle. Being led through the heart opens the path to creativity and wisdom.

You too can enter the flow, but you will need to start at the beginning, with others. Start by asking yourself these questions.

- What are my distractions?
- What are my resistances to vulnerability?
- How easily am I able to be with tension, discomfort, and disappointment?
- What helps me experience the presence of grace?
- What keeps me from living in that presence?

FEELING INTO CONNECTION

The line between science and religion is disappearing, and a vast frontier of hope is unfolding. We sense that we too might be able to let go of our own small views and explore, in fresh new ways, the possibility of living life as adventure.

In his book *Into the Magic Shop*, James R. Doty, a neurosurgeon, writes about his quest to understand the mysteries of the brain and the secrets of the heart, and how that quest led him into the practice of meditation. In his own words:

> What research has shown is the heart sends far more signals to the brain than the brain sends to the heart—while both the cognitive and emotional systems in the body are intelligent, there are far more neural connections that go from the heart to the brain than the other way around. Both our thoughts and our feelings are powerful, but a strong emotion can silence a thought, while we can rarely think ourselves out of a strong emotion. In fact, it is the strongest emotions that will trigger ruminating or obsessive thoughts. We separate the mind as rational from the heart as relational, but ultimately the mind and the heart are part of one unified intelligence. The neural net around the heart is an essential part of our thinking and our reasoning. Our individual happiness and our collective wellbeing depend on the integration and collaboration of both our minds and hearts. [20]

When, as an elementary school student, I was shown how iron filings on a piece of paper automatically line up when a magnet is passed underneath, I was curious. This was the first tangible demonstration of how what is invisible shapes what becomes visible. Through the Heartmath Institute and its research we now know that:

> The heart generates the largest electromagnetic field in the body. The electrical field as measured in an electrocardiogram (ECG) is about 60 times greater in amplitude than the brain waves recorded in an electroencephalogram (EEG). The magnetic component of the heart's field, which is around 100 times stronger than that produced by the brain, is not impeded by tissues and can be measured several feet away from the body with Superconducting Quantum Interference Device (SQUID)-based magnetometers. We have also found that the clear rhythmic patterns in beat-to-beat heart rate variability are distinctly altered when different emotions are experienced. These changes in electromagnetic, sound pressure, and blood pressure waves produced by cardiac rhythmic activity are "felt" by every cell in the body, further supporting the heart's role as a global internal synchronizing signal.[21]

Pause for a moment and let this land on you. Take in what I've shared and consider this: *Prior to speaking one word or physically gesturing in any way, you are communicating with those around you. Through the invisible magnetic field of your heart, you are connected even though you haven't tried to be. You just aren't aware!*

If you can make another step with me, please reflect on this: The fact that each cell within your body "feels" changes in electromagnetic *waves* means that your *entire* body-brain nervous system is really a tuning fork. It feels its way into self-organization and wisdom by sensing flow or blockage. If what it feels causes fight or flight, freeze or appease, or chaos or rigidity, then organic collaboration and engagement will not materialize. But when it senses flow, other things become possible.

Several years ago, during a time when there was enough hair on my head for a barber to cut, I was sitting in a barber chair while a woman I did not know was trying to style my hair.

This was during my lunch break, and I had a limited amount of time before I needed to return to my office. She was clearly preoccupied, and I wasn't interested in conversation, so there was none.

About ten minutes into the haircut, an idea about her came into my mind, but because we didn't know each other, I ignored it. After another few moments, this idea became more like a question, and it became stronger. The funny thing about this is that the question was so out of the blue, I was embarrassed to ask it. But it persisted.

A short time later, with somewhat of a red face, I asked, "Is some important date on your mind?" This caught her off guard. She was clearly annoyed and answered, with a shortness in her voice, "What?"

Self-preservation would suggest that I not annoy this person with scissors in her hand, but by now the question was even stronger, so I timidly responded, "Is there some important date that's on your mind?" To my amazement, she paused, tilted her head toward me, and quietly said, "Who told you?"

Then I was caught completely off guard, and out of my mouth came, "What's the date?" She stepped away from me for a moment, and I worried that she was about to lose it, but as she lifted her head, I could see that a slight smile was forming on her face. She whispered, "He just asked me last night. Did he tell you?" Clearly, she had wonderful news and needed to share it with someone.

About now you might wonder, "How did this happen?" or even, "Did this really happen?" As the days passed, I wondered these same things; in fact, I wondered if my mind had simply created the story, so I chose not to mention this to anyone else, and she never cut my hair again.

A few months later while test-driving a new car for my wife, something very similar occurred, with even more pronounced results. Buying a car is one of my least enjoyable experiences and even more so when the sales person insists on a test drive and occupies the passenger seat. I don't enjoy small talk, especially with a sales person, but if I wanted to drive that car, I needed to bear the burden.

We had been driving for about five minutes, and he was using this platform to make sure I understood the car's features. Even though I already knew all about them, I was trying to be polite. This continued for a bit, and then, out of nowhere, the name Lorie came into my mind.

We continued to drive, and in the meantime, this name became more than a thought. The experience with the barber made me wonder if something similar was trying to happen. Hoping that it would go away, I started making small talk by asking him about his life.

As he warmed up to me, the name Lorie became even more real, so, acting as if we might have a common friend, I asked,

"Does the name Lorie mean anything special to you"? He quickly and clearly answered, "No."

While I hoped that would be the end of it, as you can imagine, it was only the beginning. His answer seemed much too quick, and as my confidence strengthened, I said, "Are you sure the name Lorie doesn't mean something to you"?

With this, his head dropped down, and he paused; then, he lifted it again, looked at me, and said, "Did my Dad put you up to this?"

By now my full attention had been captured by the connection that had just opened up between us, so I pulled the car to the curb on a quiet residential street, looked at him, and said, "Tell me who Lorie is."

Through tears he shared that Lorie was the mother of his child and that he had abandoned them two years earlier. Since then, he had cut off all connection to his father, a minister. His sense of shame had constructed an internal barrier between him and his child and him and his father, and now, for some unknown reason, reconnection was being offered through me. As I quietly held a space for him to weep, a new thought came to me and I said, "Your father loves you; go and see him."

These experiences and others that followed opened me up to how connected we all really are. The only separations that exist are within us. They exist within the interior structures that have formed throughout our lives to keep us safe. While I had no idea how to explain my experiences, I knew that the invisible and the visible were deeply connected, and my life shifted. My awareness was growing.

Today, I understand that we are all connected through energy, information flow, and grace—this idea of *entanglement*.

Connection isn't a concept, a process to be managed, or something that gets forged on a weekend retreat or on a ropes course. Connection is reality! It is always present and always flowing, and it either supports value or waste. It is our own false sense of separation that keeps us near the banks, in the shallow currents and eddies that spin us around and around. Just like Laura and her team, when we embrace vulnerability and intimacy, we open ourselves up to connection where potential beyond belief and organic collaboration always flow. It doesn't need to be created or managed, just entered into. Awareness is all you need, and it starts to form through vulnerability.

CHAPTER 7
THE INNER-FLUENCY CONVERSATION

Gary, the owner/CEO of several franchise food stores, was excited about the opportunity to purchase other locations at favorable prices. As a former technology CEO, he associated success with an emotion: the excitement of dynamic growth. He eagerly negotiated the purchase details, even though his company's margin and cash flow trends were unstable. Nevertheless, he pressed on. The need for *the experience of excitement* overwhelmed his common sense.

Gary's CEO personality had formed during the technology boom. Personality is our adapted self and represents how we think we need to be seen by ourselves and others to thrive. It's what we have falsely established as the basis of our self-esteem. These deep inner structures limit our ability to become all we can be. Gary's persona was a costly distraction, and greater and greater waves of his attention were devoted to trying to sustain it.

When Gary called me and said he had decided to pursue his acquisition targets, his intensity was noticeable. Intensity is the energy we are released into when all of our senses are tuned to one task. While Gary was asking me to tell him what I thought, I knew he was really asking me to support his decision. Gary needed to make a shift, so I said, "Please share your dilemma with the other CEOs in your Vistage group, and give wisdom a chance to speak."

The energy attached to his persona made it difficult for him to slow down. He initially came back with, "What are they going to tell me that I don't already know?" I told him that while I had no idea, we needed to take the opportunity to find out. His old habit of rushing forward was very entrenched, but he agreed. Gary seemed to live in the future, his attention attracted to an illusory story about how great it would be, if only . . .

The winds of life were trying to shape Gary by urging him to let go of the burden of maintaining his persona. Each time we met, he shared his frustration and his latest ideas for overcoming the mounting impasses. While I sensed that the changes he mentioned would only provide temporary distraction, I stayed with him as he wrestled with his persona and reality. Gary was trying to ignore the Collaboration, Leader Effectiveness, Execution, Value Creation, and Growth Conversations, but he couldn't ignore Connection.

A week later at his Vistage CEO group meeting, I noticed that his countenance had changed—he was ready to learn. The calm presence of vulnerability and humility had replaced the driven energy that I'd previously observed. He was ready to learn because the impasse was doing its work. Gary was moving though the struggle of his current "coil" in the presence of others.

Inner Fluency Is Awareness

Over the years, I've had the good fortune to travel on a few white-water rivers in kayaks and rafts, and I've noticed that the water flows most deeply in the center. Drifting toward the rocks and banks brings turbulence. Inner fluency is about becoming attuned to where you are in the river, the flow of life, by learning to hold awareness.

While the body-brain nervous system has the innate capacity to find and maneuver to the ground of our being, our personalities—the survival operating system that formed in our reactionary youth—usually prevents us from entering the flow. Becoming attuned to your inner flow will help you correct this wobble.

While visiting Tashkent, Uzbekistan, in 1989, I attended a wedding feast. As I observed the families and friends celebrating, I wondered what was behind the smiles that were on their faces. Since I didn't speak the Uzbek language and couldn't talk directly with them, I could only imagine what was going on within them.

Becoming fluent about the interior of your being is more empowering than you can imagine, but it's also work.

Without direct experience, a story was all I could conjure. Within companies, this same thing happens between team members as each person wonders what is going on inside the other.

Management teams have a loosely designed common business vocabulary they use to talk about progress. These outward conversations are mostly conceptual and not personal. But as we descend through Leader Effectiveness, Management Team Coherence, Collaboration, and Connection, the conversations become more and more personal. We call this the domain of inner fluency and it requires a different lexicon of ideas. Without knowing a bit about this language, you can only make up a story.

Becoming fluent about the interior of your being is more empowering than you can imagine, but it's also work. Curiosity is essential to starting this process, and I have found that reconsidering how energy is formed within you is a good beginning.

As a language, inner fluency takes you back to the time in your life when you were directly aware of the stimulations that happened within your body. Your connection to yourself was real. You didn't reflect on these stimulations, so there was no need to make up stories that could help you assign meaning to the experience. You and reality were one. Your awareness didn't need the middleware of ideas, thoughts, and stories or the "idealized self" (personality) to make safe sense of what was going on.

This solid ground still exists within you. But without strong inner fluency, it's impossible to connect to the solid ground of your true self, and management team coherence will remain marginal.

I call this inner *fluency* because my goal is for you to become more able to directly experience the movement of energy within yourself, and for you to help others do the same. Your habitual thinking, feeling, and behaving are patterns that have taken up residence in your middleware—the ego. Your analytic mind isn't much help initially because figuring this out isn't possible, and that leads to ruminating. But your true self, your essential self, will emerge into the clearing if you create a space for practice.

Richard Moss, MD, helps us better understand this path:

> The true self is not a thing we can know; it is an inexhaustible power that can carry us deeper and deeper into ourselves and into reality. How much more complete our knowledge of ourselves can become depends on how deeply we yearn to know ourselves and *how much reality we can bear before fear chases us* into a dream of our own fabrication. The limit to self-realization is set the moment we reach a fear that we experience as too great to face or an idea so compelling that we identify ourselves with it. At such a moment, we lose connection to the beingness of *human being* and become only human.[22]

Recognizing how our awareness can create a new conscious relationship to any feeling, emotion, or limiting belief is one of the most empowering experiences I've had, and I'm not alone. In one way or another, each of the wisdom traditions finds its footing here.

Learning to be present with the sensations that threaten us and the feelings that carry our energy away is the path to a new inner relationship with ourselves. This is how we become more able to be present with reality and help others be there too. As we become fluent, we transform, and from here we can transcend. The scale of our being far and away exceeds our rational mind. Einstein said as much: "No problem can be solved from the same level of consciousness that created it."

Learning to bear reality to greater and greater degrees is your work.

We have an unlimited capacity for awareness. This ability to be in relationship *to* and not identified *with* whatever we are feeling is within us. When we are *aware* of our unhappiness, the presence within us that is *aware* is not unhappy. When we are *aware* of fear, that awareness is not itself afraid. Being present to reality is a leadership requirement. *Learning to bear reality to greater and greater degrees is your work.*

Inner Fluency Is Bearing Reality

My monthly meetings with Gary were a space for relationship where he could unpack his challenges, successes, and disappointments in a confidential setting. Through our times together, it became clear to me that he was blocking many possibilities in his rather rigid and unvoiced commitment to seeing himself through his technology identity. Yet I had the faith that as long we held onto our relationship, our connection, other possibilities could still emerge. Yes, I could have told Gary what I thought he needed to do, but that would be robbing him of a learning opportunity.

Gary had a "feeling" of being blocked and cut off from what he wanted. He felt terrible. As his frustrations mounted, his interior impasse became more intense and his need for release almost caused him to make a short-sighted decision. Sound at all familiar?

I knew that Gary valued the purpose of his Vistage CEO group, which is all about transformation through relationship, so when I asked him to share his dilemma with them, I knew he would. Powerful purpose is part of the ground a group stands on and it always creates a strong bond that collaboration and connection can flow through. The bond of connection is an invisible field that can be fed. It can become weak or strong.

By providing a thoughtful written description of his dilemma prior to the meeting and asking for help, Gary fed the field. By turning his back as others talked about him and his dilemma in the meeting (a process called "the box," which I'll explain in more detail later in this chapter), Gary opened to the flow with an intention to bear reality. By writing down what he heard them saying, without rebuttal or explanation, Gary accepted love.

This experience caused a shift to occur within Gary and the group, and from what had seemed like a very hard situation, a clear and a simple way forward emerged.

THE SPIRAL OF GROWTH
Within our conversational model, below the Collaboration Conversation are Connection, Inner-Fluency, and the Work Conversations.

As each conversation takes place within us, we know that others have some incomplete sense of what is going on inside us and that they are trying to make sense of it, even though these internal conversations are not visible. Connection and organic collaboration are constrained or empowered by our level of awareness and our own ability to learn to give voice to it. As awareness increases, inner fluency increases, and the quality of all conversations improves because we are more able to bear reality.

The power of our attention becomes vital here. By building the attention muscle we can begin to meet the untamed emotions that have driven us away from our true selves. We can begin to observe the stories we use to avoid feelings and learn to disengage from them by moving toward and being with them. This frees our attention to be in support of our best intentions. This is how we win! This is how the insidious patterns that have invisibly sidetracked us for years let go!

With the help of his Vistage CEO group, Gary allowed the tension to do its work. It took a while for his technology persona to dissolve, but as he stayed with the tension, a new possibility emerged.

His personality saw employees as a means to an end and caused him to experience them as a problem. As this conversation ripened, he began to see employees as humans. This emerged as he accepted himself as human, with all of his gifts, capabilities, and imperfections, in the presence of others.

As his own wholeness ripened, one day he shared, saying, "I'm beginning to see this thing I had called a 'company' as a garden. I've been focusing on the weeds. But if I focus my attention on helping the garden become a place of beauty and health, the weeds get less and less of my attention."

The Spiral of Growth demonstrated in the following illustration is evident in all of nature and throughout the universe. From ascent to descent, it's the way things are. As Gary surrendered into descent, he opened. Maintaining his artificial identity forced him to see others as the problem, so he separated himself from them. Like many of us, he had exported his problem onto others, but as humility emerged, he quit clinging to that part of his false identity and released himself into the waters of chaos where his personality could dissolve a bit. Because he was connected with a group that held a sacred space for him, he encountered the truth, and the truth began to set him free. He moved toward harmony and integration by knowing and accepting himself more deeply. With the help of others, Gary was flowing to the center of his being. In this place of solid ground, his soul was strengthened.

Richard Moss, MD, uses the metaphor of a sugar cube to describe descent. If you place the cube in a glass of water, it slowly begins to lose its shape as it descends until, eventually, there is no cube. But the essence of sugar remains. Our idealized self is like the sugar cube. No matter how hard we try to use high levels of activity, both mental and physical, to maintain form and hide from our fear, those around us know we are flailing. All the while, underneath the fear and anxiety that fuel our frenetic energy spend is a deeper, truer, much more spacious and wise presence, waiting for us to let go. This is how our essence begins to shine through.

We are taught that speed and confidence are traits of success and that rest is a sign of sloth. Our Puritan work ethic tells us to keep a stiff upper lip, and too often it's a health crisis or a loss of spouse or key employee that helps us wake up. There is an exit door from every closed circle—from every impasse, if you will—but let your heart lead you to it. Instead of prison, you will find pasture, and you will move in a spiral. The spiral is how all growth happens. But remember, the spiral moves in both directions.

After we've accumulated enough cycles as a leader, we start to see that the *spiral of growth* is really a picture of our own inner

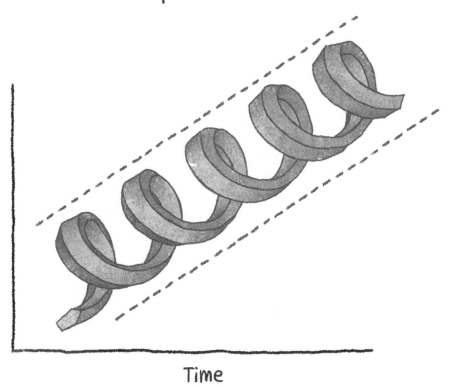
The Spiral of Growth

story. Each new spiral begins with strong upward movement. To discover that we can make a difference and that our presence seems to matter is invigorating.

Secretly, we might begin to believe that far greater possibilities could also exist for us. Ascent starts to become a part of our lived experience, and we naturally embrace ascent as "what is good."

But, while success motivates us to invest more of our energy using our historical leadership patterns, descent eventually arrives. Hopefully, as constraints increase and the personal limits of our own self-knowledge show, we ask for help, or others insist we change.

Living from Your Center

Anyone who knows Gary would say he's bright, witty, charismatic, and experienced, but to those in his Vistage CEO group, Gary would also be known as someone who is easily triggered. Gary's work was to become more integrated, to allow his heart and his body to balance his thinking. Thinking at its best can sift, sort, prioritize, categorize, construct a future, and conceptualize it; but, by itself, it cannot navigate the current. Using thinking to navigate this inner current is like using an outboard motor to turn an aircraft carrier. Thinking is logical, while being is experiential. Developing a *felt sense* requires dropping into the current. Thinking tries to keep us dry.

Integration happens when we have the courage to descend into the reality of the human experience and stay there until we become thoroughly familiar with ourselves.

Thinking is a tool for convergent problem solving and planning, but no one follows you because of logic. People either follow you because they are attracted and inspired by your heart or because they fear going against the grain.

What's inside you shows on the outside. If you use thinking as your tool of preference, others experience you as distant and controlling. If you use feelings and emotions to control the situation around you, people experience you as disruptive. If you use your sensing to be the smartest person in the room, no one else will emerge to lead, and you will be overwhelmed with responsibility.

Integration happens when we have the courage to descend into the reality of the human experience and stay there until we become thoroughly familiar with ourselves. By doing this, we develop the viscosity to move beyond the states of rigidity and chaos. We do it by naming the patterns that have held us so long. You must name them and claim them to tame them. Humility ultimately integrates the head, heart, and body into one unified presence that others want to follow.

Living from your center means getting to know the feel of the current of the river that flows within you. Paying attention to the body-brain nervous system as it shares its experience is the launching place of inner fluency.

When we can bring our attention to the ways we habitually relate to change, we become practitioners of what it means to be alive. We let the tension form us!

THE NECESSITY OF TENSION/STRUGGLE

You may have heard the story of the man who found the cocoon of an Emperor moth and took it home so he could watch the moth come out of the cocoon. On the day a small opening appeared, he sat and watched the moth for several hours as the moth struggled to force its body through that little hole.

Then it seemed to stop making any progress. It appeared as if it had gotten as far as it could and could go no farther. It seemed stuck. Then the man, in his kindness, decided to help the moth, so he took scissors and snipped off the remaining bit of the cocoon. The moth emerged easily.

But it had a swollen body and small, shriveled wings. The man continued to watch the moth because he expected that, at any moment, the wings would enlarge and expand to be able to support the body, which would contract in time. Neither happened! In fact, the little moth spent the rest of its life crawling around with a swollen body and shriveled wings. It never could fly.

What the man, in his haste, did not understand was that the restricting cocoon and the struggle required for the moth to get through the tiny opening were the Creator's design. The moth's struggle would force fluid from its body into its wings so it would be ready for flight once it was freed from the cocoon. The capacity for flight would take shape through the struggle. By depriving the moth of its transformational struggle, he deprived the moth of becoming what it was meant to be. The man's inability to bear reality cost the moth its true self. The joy of seeing the moth fly was lost to the man as well.

The constraints within each of our conversations are designed to help you and your management team fly, but if you ignore one or avoid the tension, the wobble will set in.

In our spiral of growth, the movement through ascent and descent are normal. But, like the man who clipped the cocoon to relieve the pressure, we engineer situations and distractions to keep the wobble away, rarely looking inside ourselves with the help of others. Descent is the gift that can sponsor transformation.

Persona is powerful but feels thin. It's like a Teflon coating that shifts the conversation away from our reality. It's very fragile, and when confronted directly, it fights for its life. But just as in Gary's case, real life can help you go deeper and overcome persona. Ignoring the opportunity puts you at risk of creating a morass of challenges by moving forward.

Noticing the rigor of old patterns takes courage and the help of others. We can't sustain the old habit of feeling good about ourselves only when exciting levels of growth are on the horizon, but that doesn't prevent us from investing our strength in trying.

We have a marvelous capacity called "attention," but most of us don't understand it, so we squander it, allowing it to dissipate through distraction. Try to notice what your attention is attracted to.

To many, success is so addictive that trying to hold everything together is the norm. But the limits of our own resources slowly convince us that trying harder isn't enough. Judy Brown's poem, *Trough*, captures the essence of this journey.

There is a trough in waves,
A low spot
Where horizon disappears
And only sky
And water
Are our company.
And there we lose our way
Unless
We rest, knowing the wave will bring us
To its crest again.
There we may drown
If we let fear
Hold us within its grip and shake us
Side to side,
And leave us flailing, torn, disoriented.

But if we rest there
In the trough,
Are silent,
Being with
The low part of the wave,
Keeping
Our energy and
Noticing the shape of things,
The flow,
Then time alone
Will bring us to another
Place
Where we can see
Horizon, see the land again,
Regain our sense
Of where
We are,
And where we need to swim.[23]

Trying harder seems to be a standard practice for keeping the fear and anxiety of descent at bay. Asking for help doesn't come easily for many of us, so staying busy is a common coping strategy—one that, unfortunately, prevents vulnerability from doing its work and keeps us flailing around, trying to climb the wave.

Inner Fluency Is the Journey of Transformation

Within our Vistage CEO group, we sometimes use an exercise called "the box" to help members present challenging dilemmas to their group. In preparation, members provide a written description of their dilemma in advance. At the meeting they turn their back to the group while the group has a conversation about them and their dilemma. This helps the group be much more frank because they aren't reacting to the members' body language. This is the exercise Gary did with his group when he experienced vulnerability.

That day, Gary opened the door of faith, and he began to bear impatience. When Gary turned his back to the group as they discussed him and his dilemma, he maintained hope by staying open, by listening to learn, and by bearing reality. And when the group patiently asked Gary a few deep questions, luminosity shifted Gary's perspective. This was an experience of love. He was filled by a source beyond himself. Receiving love is a profound shift!

Love is a much greater force than information. Love is a vulnerable experience that occurs when we freely receive what others have to offer. Receiving love is very difficult for most of us, and especially so for leaders. We often become leaders to avoid vulnerability.

Asking for help is much different from clicking on Google or reading this book. Help is a step toward vulnerability in the presence of others. When we ask for help, we open the door to possibilities, and we soften the nearly hard-wired persona that wants desperately to survive and keep us locked in our doom loop. We allow the sugar cube to dissolve, first around the edges, and then completely.

Songwriter Leonard Cohen tells us that there is a crack in everything, and this is how the light gets in. Without vulnerability, there can be no transformation.

When we allow faith, hope, and love to carry us forward, we enter the journey of transformation. It's like an invisible current that carries us back to our center—that authentic place of depth and resilience that allows us to be present with reality. It's the place where luminosity and wisdom reside, where being who we really are is more than enough.

Jung called this current *the Unconscious*. Native Americans call it *Wakan-Tanka* (the Great Spirit), and the Buddhists call it *Dharmakaya* (the stream of suchness). Some call it the *Tao*, while others call it the *Holy Spirit*.

Whatever name you give it, know that if you dare to enter it, you will learn to be carried to the center. Your strength and resilience will grow, and this journey will seem more purposeful. Faith opens the door to believe that this current is there, even though we don't see it.

In the days that followed Gary's breakthrough meeting, he sent out notes of thanks that expressed his sense of relief and freedom. We can feel the field if we pay attention. Our felt sense of the state of our being will always lead us into wisdom unless we isolate ourselves. The mind of the group sensed the flow and opened to it. Staying in relationship is vital. The shift to harmony and connection is what Gary felt, but for transformation to show up, he first needed to experience rigidity and chaos.

Gary's accumulated lifelong filters activated his reactive patterns. He needed his Vistage CEO group to help him see these filters clearly. Each of us needs groups. They are elementary parts of our survival. Throughout our lives, we use groups to form and re-form who we are. Groups are where our being and becoming take place. In one sense, it helps to think of groups as containers where we are shaped and transformed.

Regardless of how you see your family, it was your first container. From the moment you received your mother's milk, you embraced giving and receiving. You gave her a deep sense of mothering, and you received sustenance and love. Groups are the basis for our survival and our growth. We all need groups.

We are meant to move through groups as our longing to find our way into the highest expression of our unique life quietly draws us into becoming. We linger in groups because we gain a sense of ourselves and what's possible for us. The giving and receiving that takes place within your group is meant to strengthen your sense of self and to stretch you to become.

Just as the filters that had formed within Gary no longer served him, we each come to a time where impasses start to accumulate, and we wrestle with letting go.

I left Iowa and my family at nineteen, and my Vietnam experience took place within a container that believed in me and stretched me. They gave me the gift of intellectual rigor. My university container took place within another group, one that defined academic and business success for me. Xerox gave me a container that defined financial success—they taught me how to win.

When I think about my life through the lens of the groups that have been central to my formation, I begin to understand that longing, belonging, being, and becoming are constants throughout life. I now know that I've been drawn by an invisible current, one that I've come to trust, called love.

Each group has made a vital deposit within me, yet none define me. We are not meant to camp out with one group forever, yet we can carry the best of what each group has given us into becoming. When we feel like a group is defining us, we can also be assured that a deeper set of life-giving questions is available right below the surface, if we but linger and ask, seek and knock.

We cannot manufacture organic collaboration because it flows through connection. And organic connection only flows when we, and the rest of the management team, start to own the state of our interior life.

Gary's CEO group is a place of discovery where deep questions are meant to draw members into insights that create more solid ground. It's a place where being and becoming flourish. It's part of Gary's solid ground where exploring and risk-taking are normal.

We cannot manufacture organic collaboration because it flows through connection. And organic connection only flows when we, and the rest of the management team, start to own the state of our interior life.

Each new temporary coil in the spiral of growth includes ascent and descent. Certainly, every company experiences this, but so does every leader and employee. How do we know where we are personally in this cycle? This question plays a vital role in achieving sustainability.

As you and I exchange ideas through our interaction with this material, you might pause and linger, then gently ask yourself, *Why am I reading this? What within me is seeking new insights or answers? What is changing? What is confusing? What patterns keep coming up through me that no longer serve me, that have now become life-draining? What am I needing to attend to but don't know how?*

As the shift to descent takes form, these questions become more intense. Descent is a place to gain clarity and rest, but we cannot do this alone. To a management team that shares vulnerability, descent is the place where authentic connection and collaboration are formed, where they become more effective and durable.

As we begin to accept the most challenging questions, our interior life and the life of our management team can be transformed during descent. But if we close off and separate from our interior life and each other, the unanswered questions that are trying to help us set the stage for more impasses to accumulate. *The quality of the conversation governs the rate of adjustment.*

Inner Fluency Creates Solid Ground

Your interior is where your ground is. It's the place you make sense and meaning from the experience of each moment. The ground of your interior, your being, manifests itself in each interaction. Each time you interact with others, they experience you as "a presence." What type of presence are you bringing? Are you able to bear reality enough to discover the answer? Creating value for others with each interaction is a potent leadership purpose.

On your journey from being to becoming, you will encounter people and groups who can help or hinder your movement toward becoming grounded. Leaders who are becoming more integrated help others become more integrated. They become and create solid ground that is sustainable.

In his book *Presence and Encounter*, Dr. David Benner, an internationally known psychologist, transformational coach, author, and wisdom teacher offers insight that can help us understand presence. By understanding two specific styles of presence you can become better equipped to understand the way people participate in collaboration.

Leaders who operate primarily within a persona—an image they have constructed in support of their role—have very limited self-knowledge. Benner describes this as *confused presence* and he believes this is the most difficult presence to read. These people are unaware that managing their image drains much of their energy. A need for control is often the source of this behavior style.

When we notice that a leader's full attention isn't available, it's because it is scattered over many things that occupy their mind. The many conversations that are running through their mind are a constant distraction. Benner describes this as *preoccupied presence*. I've discovered that the spouses of many CEOs experience them as preoccupied. There is no experience of stillness or groundedness, and therefore, no capacity for real connection or collaboration.[24]

Being connected to others is how we navigate to the more solid ground of authentic presence. Others sense in our presence things that we do not see, and they can help us gain self-knowledge if we let them. We can also pay attention to our *felt sense* of others and help them, but only when giving and receiving are above board and in play. When they are, we enter the dance of life and with this we step into the flow of value creation and we flourish together

There is no better way to understand collaboration and flow than through the work of Dr. Dan Siegel. Dr. Siegel is a clinical professor of psychiatry at the UCLA School of Medicine, founding co-director of UCLA's Mindful Awareness Research Center, founding co-investigator of the UCLA Center for Culture, Brain, and Development, and executive director at the Mindsight Institute. By drawing together facts and data from decades of brain research, psychotherapy, religious traditions, mysticism, metaphysics, biology, and quantum physics, he offers a working definition of the mind as: " a self-organizing emergent property of energy and information flow happening within you and between you, in your body, and in your connections with others and the world in which we live."[25]

That's a mouthful, so, first, let me assure you that understanding this will help you become more open to shifting the way you view yourself and those you work with and help you lead a more meaningful leadership life.

Dr. Siegel is telling us that within you and between you and others, a constant flow of energy and information *emerges from beyond you*, and that flow allows you to organize it. Leading becomes more about managing your awareness and learning to facilitate flow for yourself and others. Value creation relates to how well you and your management team shape energy and information through collaboration. The type of presence you bring matters!

Here is a summary of Dr. Siegel's insights, which we will apply to our idea of inner fluency:

- Energy and information are always flowing to us from beyond and to each other.
- Self-organizing is always happening, but we can impair it.
  - o The conversations detailed in this book facilitate flow and self-organization.
- Awareness channels the movement of energy and information within and between us. By practicing our conversations we strengthen awareness.
- The physiology of our emotions, thoughts, attention, behavior, and relationships relate to the integrative fibers of the brain.
  - o We shape the integration of the brain through conversation—through the integration of our relationships
- Self-regulation correlates to the quality of our neural integration. Our brain can be *shaped by collaboration*.
  - o The conversations detailed in this book shape this.

- When you are moving in an integrated flow, you have a sense of *being* whole, full, at ease, receptive, and centered. Integration is the source of the experience of harmony.
- Changes in our emotional state correlate with a change in our level of integration. The reaction of fight, flight, freeze, or appease means our level of integration is decreasing while a grounded presence means it is increasing. The emotional states of chaos, rigidity, and harmony relate to our level of brain integration.

FAITH, HOPE, AND LOVE ALLOW THE LIGHT IN

I hesitate to use *faith, hope, and love* as a heading because the meaning has been lost through years of cultural misuse, but I can't think of a better way. This is how inner fluency grows.

Faith is about opening to a possibility beyond the tangible, the visible. Hope is holding on with patience and staying open, while love is about allowing another source to fill us to meet our need.

The story about the Emperor moth is about faith, hope, and love. Faith would have waited for nature to do its work, but the energy of impatience flooded the psyche and the cocoon was clipped, deleting hope. Love is a bit trickier. Was it loving to clip the cocoon and prevent the struggle that was trying to force the fluid of life into the wings, so the beautiful creature could become what it was meant to be? Possibly, but in hindsight, we can see that impatience robbed the joy of life from this creature. Bearing reality is a critical leadership trait and comes from a higher level of brain integration.

Let's face it, impatience is a stumbling block that many CEOs and management teams trip over. It's why so few leaders develop other leaders, and it's the reason the cycle of growth becomes a doom loop. We become stuck in one coil. Management teams fail to cultivate faith when they react to the conversational constraints that are meant to free them from old patterns by fleeing discomfort and allowing the old patterns to win.

Each coil is meant to sponsor the journey from being to becoming. Just as with the story of the Emperor moth, many of us fail to see our habituated, recycled patterns. Impatience closes off greater possibility. The doom loop is a closed circle that we maintain until our awareness grows. We are blind to the invisible leadership patterns that drain life from us and the company.

While Gary had been unconsciously motivated to see his people as the problem, his influence waned; but, as he let go and chose the garden, his influence grew, and now he leads his company from a much more noble and profitable place.

Linger with this for a bit. Does a person who people see as the problem foster connection and trust? I think most of us would answer no. Influence moves effortlessly through the invisible field of connection, while control requires words: explaining and convincing with intensity.

In summary, to avoid the Leader Effectiveness Conversation, Gary was clinging to growth through acquisition. Had he pursued growth while the foundation of his value-creation model was wobbly, he might have destroyed his company entirely. But, when he chose to ask for help and collaborate with the members of his Vistage CEO group, he started the process of letting go. As he let go, a more noble and, ultimately, more profitable creation in the form of a garden emerged.

To protect ourselves from vulnerability, we can use knowledge and brilliance as a shield. To protect ourselves from vulnerability, we can use humor, sarcasm, and storytelling. To protect ourselves from vulnerability, we can cling to unrealistic expectations at all costs and, for a short time, keep our false self from dissolving.

SENSING INTO OUR INTERIOR WORLD

Dan Siegel describes our interior world as existing through a bottom-up conduit and a top-down constructor.[26] Top-down means the experiences of the past are turned into generalized mental models. I've done this with my conversations. The ability to construct mental models from experience helps us become more efficient.

Each of the Outward-Moving Conversations in our model—Value Creation, Execution, Growth, Leader Effectiveness, and Management Team Coherence—are constructed by a capacity in our mind he calls "constructor." Most leaders have a strong constructor capacity.

The greatest level of inner fluency relates to noticing the signals coming from our interior—our inner teacher—and from being connected to what's beyond.

The bottom-up conduit capacity that exists within each of us is about feeling. Since we live in our body, experience is shaped by the senses that let us take in energy flow from the outside world. Dr. Siegel describes the senses this way:

> **Outward senses**: Being aware of hearing, sight, smell, taste and touch. (five senses)
> **Interior senses**: Being aware of the signals of our muscles and bones, and the sensations arising from our internal organs, such as our intestines, lungs, and heart. Science calls this interoception, for per*ceptions* of the interior. This is also called our sixth sense.

Mental activities: Being aware of emotions, thoughts, and memories. This is called our seventh sense.

Sense of connection: Being aware of things outside the body—our relationships with other people, pets, the planet, nature, God, and anything else outside or extending beyond the body. This relational sense is called our eight sense.[27]

The Quakers describe all this together as our "inner teacher."

The greatest level of inner fluency relates to noticing the signals coming from our interior—our inner teacher—and from being connected to what's beyond.

The ways we've learned about the world become embedded in the top-down mental models that shape how we make sense of life as it unfolds. If those models remain unchallenged, we continue to create our interactions with experiences that simply reinforce what we believe we are. The conversations offered in this book are meant to challenge your old mental models by creating a place to practice.

A turning point in one's life may arise when top-down filters that shape our feelings, perceptions, thoughts, and actions are suddenly broken down and shaken up, and a new bottom-up experience fills our awareness.

We need to connect with *sensation* to begin to liberate us from the potential tyranny of top-down filters that are usually hidden from awareness.

What happened with Gary and each of the people described in this chapter? They let go. Their impasses opened them to other possibilities, and they began to connect with the flow by paying attention and relaxing into sensing.

To close this chapter, reflect on these words from David Whyte:

"Vulnerability is not a weakness, a passing indisposition, or something we can arrange to do without, vulnerability is not a choice, vulnerability is the underlying, ever present and abiding undercurrent of our natural state. The only choice we have as we mature is how to inhabit our vulnerability."[28]

CHAPTER 8
SPEAKING FROM THE CENTER

I met Dennis when I was invited to work with a technology company. Dennis had been part of their management team for quite a while, so when I started working with them, patterns were well established—not just his, but the management team's patterns too.

In our 360° review conversation, I learned that Dennis came from a working-class family with an exceptionally strong work ethic. Feeling good about himself was dependent on feeling like he was outworking others.

When we talked about his need for structure and the lack of structure within the management team, I began to understand something about Dennis. During management team meetings, I noticed that Dennis used more words to communicate than anyone, and he almost never made a solid point that others could build on. I also noticed that no one brought this to his attention. The lack of structure and consistency in the management team created a scenario where Dennis never knew exactly what to be prepared for, so no one expected him to be well prepared. Given his desire to outwork everyone, he was compensating unconsciously by talking.

During one management team meeting I was observing, I asked Dennis to share his need for structure and consistency. He paused, thought about what I had asked him to do, and then proceeded. As he talked, his rate of speech slowed significantly. Pausing between statements punctuated the flow of ideas he shared, and I noticed that he had the full attention of each member. Now Dennis was contributing.

At the end of that conversation, I asked the others if they had noticed anything different. Each person commented on Dennis's rate of speech and how thoughtful he seemed, much to his surprise. This created the opportunity to share how they had previously experienced him.

His previous speech pattern was part of a management team pattern. When we talked about his rate of speech and the fact that it had bothered others for years, I asked his team, "Why didn't you ever bring it up?" The answer: "We knew how hard Dennis worked, and we didn't want to disrespect him."

Dennis and the team had been suffering through long meetings with too many words and lack of structure for too long. Their conversations rarely optimized value creation. While this reality was right in front of them, no one held the inner strength and skill to embrace it. When Dennis voiced his authentic need for structure, he spoke from his center. He authored.

Each human has a strong desire for self-expression; but, when we aren't centered, this desire becomes shallow and unattractive. Self-retrieval—the process of learning to lead from the solid ground of your center—is the antidote, and that day, Dennis crossed a threshold. In future management team meetings, he paused and connected with his center before he spoke. A permanent shift! That day, Dennis was speaking from his heart. His attention had been regathered.

To become more sustainable leaders, we must become adept at noticing what is going on within our interior. When a *noticing* capacity is cultivated within a management team, sustainability becomes possible.

When we speak from our center, we engage the soul and express ourselves authentically. The soul is the source of all creativity, and it thrives with risk. Dennis's risky shift helped form an ethos of freedom and depth within the management team. When the management team's patterns are hollow, all impasses originate from that emptiness. Pausing, dropping out of our heads, and breathing into our centers can become automatic.

Shifting to Center

While we'd like inner thresholds like the one Dennis encountered to have key performance indicators, metrics, and data, they never do. Yes, these critical business indicators can highlight external change, but inner thresholds are much deeper and more meaningful. While metrics give your mind more work to do, an inner threshold starts with subtle feelings and by being attentive and curious, these feelings will lead you into wisdom. The day Dennis voiced his concern and was heard, he tapped into that strength.

Because an invisible operating system holds each member of a management team in a "field" of habitual behavior, upgrading performance is challenging. Your field of habitual behavior supports the standing of each member. If you change behavior, standing can quickly deteriorate. When you are in the field, you can't see it.

An *inner shift* is required to navigate this impasse. Passing through an inner threshold is challenging when your entire focus is on the externals—others, results, conditions, how others perceive you.

Impasses form in many ways, but they generally fall into two categories that are interrelated—inner and outer. An outer impasse is easy to see and usually nothing but an issue to resolve. But when an outward issue remains unresolved, it becomes an impasse, and this almost always points to a struggle within the inner landscape of leadership. The reactive patterns, and the automatic filters they bring, have clouded perception.

By tolerating his wordiness, Dennis's management team itself was "an impasse." But when Dennis voiced his need for structure and consistency, an inner shift occurred that allowed his true self to flourish.

Until we reach a certain inner threshold, slipping back into the mental patterns that sponsored an impasse is normal. A threshold is a bit like a flywheel—it needs lots of initial energy to move it until it achieves its purpose. Part of that purpose is to create an opportunity for conversations to grow and strengthen as the members of the management team accumulate enough inner awareness to lift off into reality. Usually, this means you will encounter some suffering. Until there is enough inner force to be open to reality, the impasse continues.

THE WOBBLE

My younger brother, Bob, received a top for Christmas one year— the type that has a pump handle. The faster you pump the handle, the faster the top spins. If you go fast enough, it generates a pleasing humming sound. It was a blast playing with the top and seeing how fast we could make it go, then watching the circle of its rotation widen into a wobble, until, with its energy spent, it collapsed onto its side.

When a management team continues to orbit around an impasse, their conversations remind me of the last stages of a spinning top. Just as the top struggles to hold on to its rotation, management teams divert their scarce energy to lower-priority initiatives to keep busy. Keeping busy, which often involves too many words, allows one to ignore a deep sense of inadequacy.

This illustration of the top shows us how the conversations work together to bring coherency to the management team.

Management Team Coherence Conversation

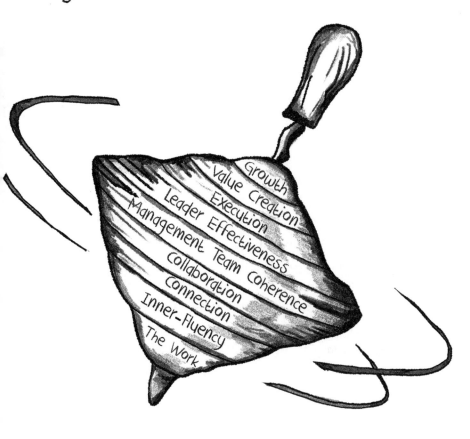

"Standing" as a member of a high-performing management team in the past was primarily based on "getting stuff done." No longer. Today it's about presence: being present to your own emotional experience so you can help the team playfully work the conversations without being sidetracked. Being sidetracked is a symptom. The root cause is inner wobble. Becoming more grounded in your center is the antidote.

Dennis's CEO, Russ, who led the management team meetings, was resourceful. He had led the company well through its startup phase into a place of national recognition for innovation, with an impressive list of nationally known customers.

Not surprisingly, as I participated in their meetings, I noticed that Russ needed to feel like he was in control, and when he felt out of control, the volume and intensity of his voice increased slightly. As I engaged with Russ, I gained a deeper understanding of the beliefs that fostered this pattern.

Just as my brother spun the top he received, Russ tried to take control—grab the "handle"—and create torque whenever he needed to soothe his anxiety. Russ's need emanated from a deep, unspoken sense of inadequacy. Whenever he felt "a wobble," his intensity increased. This ultimately served to divert the team's energy away from the impasse, helping Russ regain control. But it also cut Russ and the team off from the plane of possibilities.

In one of their management team meetings, I paused and asked Russ if we could talk about what I had observed. He agreed, so I described the pattern and asked the others to evaluate my comments. Like turtles coming out of their shells, one by one they added their sense of his pattern. Russ became anxious a few times; but, before he could reply defensively, I asked him to pause and breathe, which created space for the Leader Effectiveness Conversation to develop.

Like a flywheel slowly turning through the first revolution and more freely turning as we stayed with it, the conversation found a depth that had previously been absent. Russ made a shift in that conversation. He discovered that he was resilient enough to stay with his anxious feeling and breathe into it, without making up a story about it. He let the tension do its work, and organic collaboration surfaced. The insidious, invisible pattern that had sidetracked their team was starting to pull back.

Becoming known allows the currents of depth to flow through a connected leadership team, and you are set free from continually reaching out to scrape together affirmation, respect, and significance for yourself.

In the past, Russ's body had tensed in response to anxiety, but now he was learning to relax into it. Tensing up tends to calcify energy, thereby strengthening the reactive pattern that has formed since childhood. Relaxing and breathing into the discomfort tends to metabolize the energy, making it available for new possibility.

By talking about Russ's pattern and by each member of the management team sharing their perspective while Russ did his best to stay present, we began to unfold a more wholesome management team operating system.

BEING PRESENT, BEING KNOWN

Without being known, as humans, with all the parts and pieces that have been in hiding, our ego forages for belonging around a fragmented center, and that's what had been happening in this management team's meetings. Becoming known allows the currents of depth to flow through a connected leadership team, and you are set free from continually reaching out to scrape together affirmation, respect, and significance for yourself.

This is the stuff that most senior management teams orbit around, but when a shift emerges like the one Russ and his team embraced, intimacy paves the way for heavy-lifting and a path through impasse. We can transcend impasses as we are transformed.

All of us are dynamic. From moment to moment, newness is hoping to emerge. When a senior management team becomes capable of intimacy, a *space* for becoming takes root. Each session then becomes filled with the possibility of discovering more of who you really are and what you can do. When we embrace our humanity, our gifts become more evident and our limitations more acceptable.

When you come to know yourself in the presence of others on this same path, you become more integrated. As integration deepens, inner strength grows. Your inner fluency enables you to notice when you encounter a reactive pattern. Through our work together, Russ's team made a commitment to *noticing,* which was becoming evident in the way they *practiced* in their management team meetings. And, as a result, their capacity to create value outside of that meeting began to flourish too. The plane of possibility was opening.

A friend of mine explained that he understands intimacy as *into-me-you-see.* Intimacy always requires an increase of effort to bear it, to remain upright in the face of it. Being present to intimacy has a weight that is sometimes overwhelming. It takes great attention on the part of the soul not to give way under the weight. Transforming the habituated energy of unproductive patterns always entails inner upheaval and intimacy.

While intimacy with yourself and then with others can be terrifying, entering the clearing so you become known first to yourself and then to the management team is a path toward sustainability. The path toward truth and sustainability are the same.

Through the community-shared 360° reviews, Russ and his team had embraced the value of "getting comfortable being uncomfortable," but we were just beginning.

Getting the Sap to Flow

When I tell you that each management team I've worked with ultimately gets so comfortable being uncomfortable that they learn to have fun with it, you might think I'm exaggerating.

When a management team embraces the reality of being fully imperfect human beings, they reset not only their historical relationships, but also the way they think about value creation, execution, growth, and leader effectiveness. When the pressure to avoid discomfort is relieved, posturing and pretense soften, and the structure of the conversations begin to guide energy and information flow.

Over the years, I've discovered a variety of profiling tools including the Core Values Index, Profiles International, Myers-Briggs, and StrengthsFinder. Most of these, in the hands of a professional, are helpful pre-employment screening tools. They can help you decide whether a person is a fit. But I have found that applying these to team building yields very little long-term success. Why?

As Carl Jung said, a wall is built brick by brick, from the outside; but, in nature, growth occurs as the sap rises from the roots and the cells organically divide and multiply. The volume of sap and cellular growth create organic increase.

Team building is usually an add-on event and, therefore, just another brick. Sap doesn't start flowing through one event. In nature, the environment supplies ingredients to support the longing for growth that inherently exists within each plant, mammal, animal, or cell. Authentic growth occurs from within, and impasses are often the catalyst to creating the conditions that will allow the sap to flow and growth to flourish.

In my yard, I have several majestic Douglas fir and cedar trees. A few years back, I hired an arborist to thin and prune them to optimize their health. While the wind storms around me knock out power, forcing my generator to kick in several times each year, these trees have easily withstood the storms. Recently, I noticed that sap was freely flowing down the bark of the tree from each place the arborist had removed a significant limb. While the remaining limbs are flourishing with exceptional new growth, an excess of sap is finding its way to the surface through the wounds that were intentionally created to ensure its health. The tree is self-regulating.

When a management team begins working from the inside, each threshold they pass through exposes dysfunction and limitation. When these come to the surface, acceptance and humility flow, just like the sap from my trees. Sap naturally wants to flow, but most leaders have unconsciously blocked the path to growth.

TAPPING THE SOURCE WITH THE ENNEAGRAM
To suggest that we don't really know ourselves might seem ridiculous, but that's exactly what I'm saying. I've worked with hundreds of executives, CEOs, and managers. Without exception, each comes with a survival operating system. Yes, some are more aware, and certainly many are more open, but all have been blinded by the survival instinct that permeates their personal operating system.

Having lived most of my professional life in the technology world, I've come to appreciate how important operating systems are. Operating systems work behind the scenes. To a user, a good operating system isn't noticeable. But to a programmer, the operating system is a framework that governs possibility and limitation. Each of us lives through an invisible operating system that governs possibility and limitation.

Watch any small child and you will notice that they tend to go with whatever attracts them. They do not evaluate options. However, in the first six years of life, marked change occurs. The experiences children have in relationship to those who are most important to them shape their automatic behavior. Personality forms around our experiences of being accepted, affirmed, rejected, or frightened within the containers we are a part of. Personality develops in response to a need for survival and acceptance, but there is much more than personality to each of us.

In 2005, someone gave me a book about the Enneagram and, after spending five minutes with it, I placed it on my bookshelf for a future read. A few years later, I participated in a nine-month course called "Living from the Heart" in which the Enneagram was introduced as a resource that could help us see ourselves more clearly from the inside out.

There are different frameworks for applying the Enneagram, and my preference is the Narrative Tradition, which offers a uniquely transformative experience using interactive panel interviews.

The Enneagram is a powerful tool of self-inquiry that describes nine personality types. No one owns the rights to it and elements of it are found as far back as 1,800 years ago. In other words, it's time-tested. As a tool for personal and collective transformation, I have found it to be unmatched.

Stemming from the Greek words *ennea* (nine) and *grammos* (a written symbol), the nine-pointed Enneagram symbol represents nine distinct strategies for relating to the self, others, and the world. Each Enneagram type has a different pattern of thinking, feeling, and acting that arises from a deep inner motivation or worldview.[29]

I had Russ and his team work with the Enneagram, and through it, their reactive patterns became visible, first to themselves and then to each other. This was the first time they could see the hidden patterns that were driving their reactive behavior and creating waste.

The fun came as they noticed the reactive patterns in the others and then paused to describe recent instances that stood out. Initially, it was challenging; but, in time, each noticed these things about themselves. Showing up this way with each other in their management team conversations sponsored a deepening embrace of humility; and, through the wounds, the sap began to flow freely. Intimacy had formed.

Over time, they shared what they were learning about themselves with their spouses. In all cases, the spouses said, in effect, "You didn't know that about yourself? I've seen it for years." Intimacy always follows humility, and being humbled by truth in the presence of others is the type of wound that helps one flourish.

THE SPACE OF NOTHINGNESS

In my Vistage Key Executive and CEO groups, we also embrace the Enneagram, and our monthly meetings are founded upon the virtue of humility. What's surprising is how much this helps us have fun. We quickly notice pretense and posturing with a smile and a gentle comment. The practice of *noticing* can flourish with trusted peers.

Nothingness is the only place something truly new can emerge. If there is not a space for a plant, it will not grow. If old behaviors fill a space, new behaviors, no matter how much they are desired, are crowded out. If a space to see yourself is filled with ruminating, the self you are—your essence—will be crowded out by the constructed self you tried to become.

Almost all of us avoid nothingness—the place of imagined emptiness, the void. This unfamiliar terrain, this clearing, is different from what we imagine. I don't think it is this place itself that we fear. Rather, I think we fear what might happen if we allow the reality of this space that permeates everything to enter our consciousness.

Nothingness creates a space for surprise to show up. It allows the unexpected to enter the clearing. In most spiritual traditions, this is called *awakening*.

When Russ and his management team started the inner journey, they had no idea what to expect. In other words, the unexpected was certain to fill the space.

While they could not imagine how humbly accepting their humanity could be related to becoming more effective, something within them longed for more, and they persisted. Longing is an instinct of the soul; if we pay attention and look deeper than thoughts, feelings, reactions, and desires, we can sense our inner longings. And if we notice them and let them lead us, we discover an amazing capacity to see through ambiguity, paradox, and complexity. We begin to know simplicity, and we find strength to face reality. *Impasses simply point to filters that blind our perception.*

When you awaken to your inner simplicity, these filters begin to fall away, and we realize that the *seeing* we were trying to do was really *thinking*. We were using our intellect wrongly and that was the source of our tiredness. When your primary landscape for work is the territory of the intellect, you see nothing of new value. The intellect can simply rearrange what it knows and thinks.

The world functions through power structures, and so do companies. Russ's power structure was based on knowing, knowledge, and being verbal. Unconsciously, he had adopted the persona of being the smartest guy in the room. Can you imagine how this desire (not longing) clouded his capacity to perceive?

John O'Donohue shares that:

> There is a beautiful complexity of growth within the human soul. It is helpful to visualize the mind as a tower of windows. Sadly, many people remain trapped at one window, looking out every day at the same scene in the same way. Real growth is experienced when you draw back from that one window, turn, and walk around the inner tower of the soul and see all the different windows that await your gaze. Through these different windows, you can see new vistas of possibility, presence, and creativity. Complacency, habit, and blindness often prevent you from feeling your life. So much depends on the frame of vision—the window through which you look.[30]

As each member of the management team began to see the patterns of the others, a new window into their own patterns emerged. As each, at their own pace, accepted these as part of who they are, awareness softened the patterns, leaving space for something new to unfold. Subtly, but irreversibly, more wisdom and truth appeared, and pretense and posturing disappeared.

Allowing the Flow of Self-Organization

Neuroscientist Dan Siegel talks a lot about the principle of self-organizing. In his words, self-organizing simply emerges. We can either impair it, or we can facilitate it. This sounds a lot like John O'Donohue's words: "Through these different windows, you can see new vistas of possibility." It seems that if we get out of the way, self-organizing flows—it happens within us.

Siegel has discovered that there are three primary states of *being* that occur in each of us and which mostly determine behavior. I have mentioned these previously—harmony, rigidity, and chaos—but let's go deeper. *Harmony* is a sense of being full, whole, at ease, and receptive. *Rigidity* is a feeling of not being able to escape a sense of repetition of thought or behavior, or a loss of excitement for life. *Chaos* feels scattered, distracted, and fragmented. Clearly, rigidity and chaos limit a capacity for self-organizing, while harmony facilitates this flow.

My experiences with executive leadership correlate to the ideas of rigidity, chaos, and harmony. Within a management team, these are the states that either limit or empower. When self-organization flows, the sap flows freely.

I think all of us would agree that the key to sustainability is self-organizing in response to the issues that arise within a business, regardless of whether they emanate from internal or external conditions. With this foundation in mind, please consider the following.

When self-organizing is impaired, feelings that correlate to rigidity and chaos are noticeable. For instance, if a leader has been orbiting around an important set of results without much progress, you can be sure that feelings of rigidity, chaos, or both have been building.

On the other hand, when this same leader is part of a management team that practices humility and intimacy, the flow of help from the others is more organic and the management team's conversations self-organize in relationship to any blockages that disrupt the flow. In this case, each new disruption is an opportunity for further integration toward harmony. Noticing the feelings and talking about the flow or its disruption is all that's required. Name it to tame it. An impasse can become a signal, a catalyst of sorts, leading us back to harmony.

I've participated in thousands of meetings that left me with feelings of frustration. We all know this isn't uncommon. While these meetings certainly do need to be upgraded, what's more interesting is what's underneath frustration.

Frustration, which is low-grade anger, is simply an indicator that what was hoped for didn't happen. Most people hope for meaningful interactions in which they feel like they've contributed something that others can build on. When chaos or rigidity is present, their hopes are blocked.

I've come to believe that every human being, every employee, every leader, wants to contribute and be appreciated for it. *The test for a good meeting is contribution.*

Think about this: your company is an amazing platform. It's the one place that every person, at least initially, starts the employment journey with the unstated purpose of contributing and thereby creating meaning. As Gallup tells us, partway into this journey, more than sixty-five percent of employees no longer believe this to be possible.

Conversations are to a company as sap is to a tree. When conversations are stewarded as "contribution" events, everyone wins because everyone creates and receives value. Wobbly conversations fuel frustration, while intentional conversations accelerate the creation of meaning. Meaning fuels organic growth in people, ideas, profits, and revenue. Conversations need structure initially, but they evolve into sustainable interactions that generate growth through the intimacy and self-knowledge that create harmony.

CHAPTER 9
THE WORK

As we wrap up our discussion about leading from the edge of the inside, I hope you now understand that as leaders' interior landscapes become more sustainable, so do their companies. As awareness expands, complexity becomes less daunting and the capacity to transcend divergent problems grows.

Traditionally, management teams might describe their wobble as "not enough" growth, value creation, or execution; but, the wobbly nature of companies usually reflects the wobbly interior of the leader. Because of this, most management teams expend much of their energy reacting to their instability. This is when they gravitate toward these Outward-Moving Conversations, looking for answers.

Although the Outward-Moving Conversations are typically more comfortable for us, they can keep us away from what's personal. When pursued in-depth, each conversation has the intensity, through the potent questions they generate, to help us step away from the patterns that produce waste. Then the form that energy takes is more durable. Tension is a key ingredient to transformation and sustainability. By learning to be present to the tension, the scale of our being is transformed. This is Step One in the Work Conversation! Help each other learn to thrive in tension.

By cultivating greater spaciousness within you, energy will form less reactively and more naturally, and value creation will become higher and more meaningful for you, your employees, your customers, your suppliers, and the communities that support your company. We are all in this together!

Over the years I've noticed a pattern. Outward-Moving Conversations lack depth because of the increasing tension and anxiety that one or more leaders on the management team experience. By not asking the deeper, more challenging questions and holding the tension they create, the ground becomes wobbly. Not knowing what to do as the tension arises causes these critical business conversations to be sidetracked. Until a management team can playfully allow this tension to do its work, reacting to the wobble is normal. Being present as reality comes into view is initially difficult. Becoming the kind of leader who humbly acknowledges this while doing the work is what leadership is all about. Knowing how to do the work is important.

Each conversation in our model is partly a manifestation of all the others, so we see that the Inward Conversations around Collaboration, Connection, and Inner Fluency—which are initially nearly invisible—emerge through and are driven by the depth of the Outward-Moving Conversations. Therefore, each of these conversations is meant to become a place of practice for the management team. Practicing together is Step Two!

I've said, "I've never seen a business problem that couldn't be solved, but I've noticed that many leaders struggle to be present with reality and help others be there too." Most of the teams and leaders I've had the privilege to work alongside also hold this view now.

The illustrations I provide for each conversation are there to help you navigate the journey. These models will help you find your way into reality when you honor their constraints. They can generate an array of potent questions for management team collaboration, and they can make sure your energy is wisely stewarded. Playfully exploring the tension associated with these conversations is the work of the management team. Becoming playful as you work together through these conversations together is Step Three.

"Management team space is a place of practice."

The Growth, Value Creation, and Execution Conversations are frameworks for tackling convergent problems, which can readily be solved with the thorough application of logic, data, and analysis, provided the management team can stay with them (which is a divergent problem).

Moving further into our conversational model, divergent problems will become evident, which means that the leaders need to transcend their own patterns so that the management team can as well. They do this by playfully bringing their limiting patterns into consciousness with each other.

From this point on, it becomes important that the management team space is a place of practice. Below the surface, some level of transformation should always be underway. Helping each other become open to the tension and the corresponding possibility of transcending what seem to be very complex challenges becomes vital.

There is no limit to value creation; the only limitation is our own willingness and ability to do the work together.

At this point, inner fluency should be paramount. Step Four is to transform your management team meetings into a space for practice by practicing the conversations each time you meet.

When the Inner-Fluency and Connection Conversations within and between management team members are grounded in a growing sense of awareness through *practiced* "public conversations" and supported by tension, coherence begins to create the solid ground that allows greater and greater levels of value creation. There is no limit to value creation; the only limitation is our own willingness and ability to do *the work* together.

The Levels of Sustainability

One vital component of the work is having the right frame of reference. I find that most privately owned companies have little chance of becoming sustainable and flourishing because their frame of reference is limited. But, with new insight, sustainability becomes possible. The following illustration can help shift your frame of reference and thereby open a fresh door into new possibilities.

By embracing the Value Creation, Execution, and Growth Conversations, and by starting to practice each with your team, everyone's frame of reference begins to shift. This is how you begin the sustainability journey. Each conversation is a frame of reference, that, when explored within your team, opens to the next conversations. Staying with deeper and deeper questions until solid insights emerge is the key.

As you begin the Level I process, initially you will notice that a new quality of concentration is required and that this takes willpower. Eventually, though, the need for willpower will dissipate, and concentration will become effortless.

The Leadership Spiral of Growth
Achieving Sustainability by Practicing Conversational Integrity

Level of Sustainability	The Conversations
I	Value Creation Execution Growth
II	Leader Effectiveness Management Team Coherence
III	Collaboration Connection
IV	Inner-Fluency

As you stay with practicing in a light-hearted way, a desire to explore Leader Effectiveness and Management Team Coherence will naturally emerge. With this you enter Level II.

While Level I brings a quality to concentration that requires little effort, Level II draws you and your team further into the Spiral of Growth by introducing vulnerability. As you and your team allow the Level II conversations and their questions to help you practice being vulnerable, you will notice that connection and collaboration are forming.

Practicing the Level II conversations creates the space for the Level III conversations to emerge naturally. By deploying your newly found powers of concentration, combined with an expanding capacity for vulnerability, the experience of Connection and Collaboration become awkwardly evident, as a feeling. Each of the illustrations related to these conversations are designed to help you move quickly into more productive and fulfilling frames, so use the illustrations to shift from feeling to thinking as you practice.

The Level III illustrations and your experience of practicing them will put you in touch with the inner experience of yourself as the tension does its work. Talking about your experience together with greater and greater levels of freedom is how we enter Level IV.

Ultimately, the Level I, II, III and IV conversations become automatic as deeper and more meaningful questions capture your curiosity. Integrity is forming.

Before the conversations, reality was viewed as "out there." After, we don't look out at reality as if it's hidden in the distance. We look out from reality. At this point, your personal viewing platform is centered.

Sustainability and conversational integrity go hand in hand. With practice your company can become sustainable, and with this, your leadership journey can become more meaningful and enduring.

The Current of Affect

The business and technology media are filled with speculative interviews and editorials about the impending societal disruption associated with artificial intelligence, blockchain, 3-D printing, driverless cars, augmented reality, the cloud, and 5G. While these are important, another much quieter revolution is underway regarding *awareness*. While the above disruptions are occurring in the outer world, this revolution is taking place within.

The research of Lisa Feldman Barrett, Distinguished Professor of Psychology at Northeastern University, and her team will help us gain an understanding of this revolution within. According to Barrett,

> Other people regulate your body budget too (how your body allocates its resources). When you interact with your friends, parents, children, lovers, teammates, therapist, or other close companions, you and they synchronize breathing, heartbeats, and other physical signals, leading to tangible benefits.[31]

Barrett goes on to explain *affect,* which is a general sense of feeling that you experience through each day. It is not emotion, but a much simpler feeling with two features. The first is how pleasant or unpleasant you feel. The second feature is how calm or agitated you feel, which is called arousal. Anytime you have an intuition that an investment is risky or profitable or a gut feeling that someone is trustworthy or an asshole, that's also *affect*. Even a completely neutral feeling is affect. Affect is a constant current throughout your life, even when you are completely still or asleep.[32]

The *current* Barrett describes takes the millions of interior stimulations flowing through your body-brain nervous system each day and associates them with the conclusions from your past that are wired into your neuropathways. These conclusions are called concepts and categories, and they have been building since very early childhood.

In one sense, these "structures" are very helpful because they efficiently help you make snap decisions without thinking. On the other hand, though, these same structures are what have formed into your personality, which is completely reactive. They make it very difficult to remain open and curious—exactly what's needed to navigate the Outward-Moving and Inward Leadership Team Conversations.

Remaining open is the path to sustainability. Given that "affect" is a "current" that is present each moment of each leader's life, learning to notice this during the Outward-Moving and Inward Conversations becomes useful. Doing the work to increase awareness is vital to becoming a sustainable leader. As I've worked with this principle in my Vistage CEO group, their understanding of affect began to expand.

James A. Russell of the NIH has developed the following illustration that I have found very useful.[33]

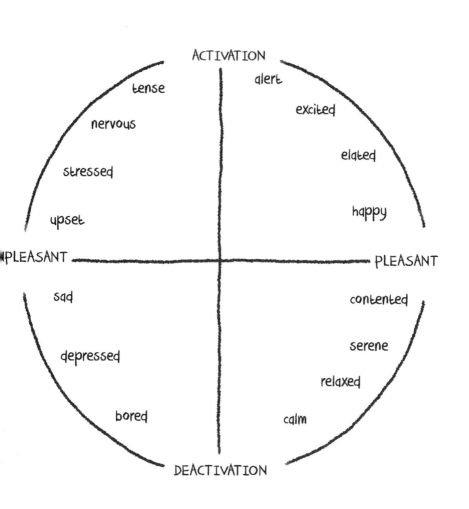

The central idea here is that we each make automatic cognitive interpretations of core neural sensations (subtle feelings). The two dimensions—unpleasant to pleasant and activation to deactivation—shed light on why many of our leadership conversations become sidetracked. I've noticed that some leaders facilitate meetings and conversations in a way that only allows for the upper right quadrant categories. Others who tend to be somewhat intimidating try to keep the upper left quadrant categories active. Surprisingly, I've also noticed that many leaders struggle with the lower right quadrant categories. Almost none can stay with or tolerate the lower left quadrant.

Consider your own preference. I've asked my CEOs to place an X over those that they resist most and to circle those they are most attracted to. Step Five is to do this together as a management team and share with each other. By doing this you will come a step closer to getting to know yourself. Growing in your ability to be present with all of these conversations is liberating and a basis for leading from solid ground. Without this self-knowledge, you will continue to be sidetracked.

The current of affect primarily comes from prediction. Barrett suggests that everything you feel is a prediction based on your past experiences. You might think you are a rational creature, but the structure of your brain makes this implausible.

Your brain is wired to listen to your body budget (the subtle feelings of inner sensations that Dan Siegal mentioned). *"Affect is in the driver's seat and rationality is a passenger."*[34] Barrett goes on to explain that it doesn't matter whether you're choosing between two snacks, two job offers, two investments, or two heart surgeons—your everyday decisions are driven by a loud-mouthed, mostly-deaf scientist (predictor) who views the world through affect-colored glasses.[35]

Your body and your brain are invisibly running on predictions until you start to wake up. Once you start "the work" and stay with it, your historical patterns soften, allowing you to remain more and more open and present. Being present with reality allows you transcend divergent problems. This is how you form leadership mastery.

Doing the Work

Ultimately, doing the work and embracing tension holds everything in balance. When a non-reactive presence begins to show up within each management team conversation, solid ground replaces the wobble and makes it much easier to maintain forward momentum.

Twenty-first century psychology, neuroscience, and contemplative religions are developing a new scholarly research category called contemplative neuroscience.[36] As science has deployed increasingly sophisticated tools, it is confirming what contemplatives within each religious tradition have been intuiting for thousands of years. Scientists and thousands of leaders within Christianity, Buddhism, Hinduism, and Taoism now acknowledge that our higher nature rests upon a necessary foundation of our lower nature and that the path of becoming present to and living and leading through our higher nature starts by becoming acutely aware of how our lower nature, with its patterns *Taking and giving energy is what we are actually doing.* and structure, has been formed. The "currents" of energy that flow within you are regulated by patterns that were formed in childhood. By bringing this into awareness and accepting that we each are fully human, a journey into wholeness unfolds.

We respond to each other's energy more than exact words or actions. Taking and giving energy is what we are actually doing. Energy is received or deflected based on its quality and starting to notice how you respond or react can help you peer more deeply into your patterns.

THE WORK OF BEING FULLY HUMAN

Dick, a management team member, longed to stay in the upper right category of feelings. He and his peers seemed to enjoy each other, but whenever high-value conversations developed, tension and anxiety led Dick to create just enough distance to remain safe. Dick was sophisticated. His sense of humor, timing, and ability to allow others to step forward created safety but also artificially limited his contribution. His shallow connection to his center created wobbly ground, so his standing within the group was somewhat tentative, though no one would have said so. To flourish, he needed to curiously embrace his patterns of protection and explore how they formed. By bringing this into his conscious awareness, Dick became more whole and his contribution jumped.

Like Dick, every family has a vague set of changing rules that are not in writing. In fact, the script for my participation in my family, from the time of gestation on, emerged day by day as my parents and three brothers reacted to each other and their external social settings in the process of trying to belong *and* get their needs met. As John O'Donohue tells us, "The human heart is a theater of longing. One of our deepest longings is to find love and friendship."[37]

Within our families, the creative tension between longing and belonging is fierce, and from this social reality we unconsciously map into our neural pathways the structure of our personality. Personality is a map of the social reality we experienced in the container of our family. This same tension is at work within our management teams, and by bringing it into our consciousness, we begin to relax our group mind so that transformation can unfold.

Transformation is possible because underneath our superficial longings is a deeper longing within each of us for self-discovery. *Who am I? What am I capable of? Who can help me discover this?* Limits are real but are meant to be temporary. They are meant to call us beyond–into another field of experience through relationship.

LONGING TO BELONG

A pattern of longing, belonging, and tension is present in every part of life, every day, just as it should be; and, within this nearly overwhelming stream of stimulation, the brain automatically wires itself to function so the body can maintain interior balance. Within whatever environment the brain finds itself, it wires itself, in direct response to stimulation. The human brain is a cultural artifact because it is wired by experience. [38]

The word *belonging* is meaningful because it contains two foundational components of life. It holds the tension of *being* and *longing*, and within this tension our patterns form. We journey through life searching for where, with whom, and how to belong. This is why we embed ourselves unconsciously in unproductive containers, the socially constructed relationships we call groups. Each of us starts within our family, no matter how functional or dysfunctional it is.

Each moment of life, our body-brain nervous system is bombarded with sensations. As a newborn, we experience these sensations directly, but as children with a functioning reflective capacity, we embrace the concepts and categories of our families to "make sense." If we didn't make sense of these sensations, they would overwhelm us. We do this in our brains through concepts, categories, and stories that we automatically create from the social reality of the groups we are in. Groups are where we form almost all of our personality.

Recently, I asked the fourteen members of my Vistage Key Executive group to take a few minutes and list the important groups they had been a part of from birth up to that day. While the average was twenty-four, one person could remember forty-eight, while another listed eight. The most important part of this exercise was learning about what they had received from each group and why they moved on. Groups are to a person as the womb is to a fetus.

The womb is the place where intimacy between man and woman creates a third, entirely new being. Similarly, belonging also holds creative possibility. In the groups and management teams I've been working with, members form and transform, "greening" takes place. In today's culture, work is a primary focus, yet very few of us have conceived of it as a place for "greening" ourselves from the inside. While skill acquisition is important, greening happens from the inside out. Skill acquisition is an outside-in move.

Unfortunately, in most management teams, by sidestepping the tension, we conform in order to maintain our standing. Just like Dick, our personalities (our lower and necessary nature) help us conform to a relatively low level of social reality. Our constructed sense of self has invisibly helped us to safely maintain our standing, but the wobbly ground we stand on also holds us back from becoming all we are meant to be. This is the tension that I hope you will embrace.

The thread that has been running through my mind for years is how to help us reframe the way we think about privately owned companies so that they better help each of us become who we really are at our core—our higher nature. In my work with management teams, we always start by recognizing that how we participate in groups determines who we become. This is the foundation for our work together. Longing to belong is the most powerful of all human longings. We only gain an authentic sense of belonging when we are known and truly seen by those in our group. Important groups can be family, neighbors, sport teams, churches, or a variety of other forms. Here we are focused on the management team. I believe we move from group to group to group in search of being seen and known, which is how connection forms. We unconsciously want to discover what we are capable of because that will help us discover who we are. Becoming all we are intended to be is the invisible thread of longing that draws each of us together.

Beneath rumination is a unique destiny that we each have been created for. Longing reaches into the gap between what is and what's desired. It tries to create the solid ground of risk-taking and exploration—ground that is necessary to become all we were meant to be.

In the early stages of this journey, we all depend on the affirmation and affection of others to awaken our ability to love ourselves. But our sense of self should not depend on receiving this from the outside. If it does, we remain trapped within the prison of our constructed self, always working for just enough affirmation, recognition, and respect. Dysfunctional containers thrive this way. Until the core of who we each are can show itself, we remain trapped. Our true selves long to explore. Listen to your longing. It will lead you to spaces where inner freedom is prized.

How do I connect to myself and others in the shared spaces of my life? This is one of the most important questions you can ask. My purpose in writing this book is to help you create a thriving management team container that flourishes through organic collaboration within and between members.

How you connect to yourself and others on your management team is usually an outside-oriented experience that is manifested by a set of external results or problems. What I've discovered is that by developing inside experience, we accelerate value creation. But more important, we experience a much greater sense of meaning because the space called "work" sees us for who we truly are and are becoming. In this process, we begin to experience greater inner freedom.

Connect to Yourself and Others in Shared Space

Dick was the fifth person on the management team to share the experiences of his life through our life-inquiry practice. Because he had witnessed the freedom that the others had experienced, courage came to him. For Dick, belonging meant opening a risky door into greater inner awareness and contribution.

Kathleen Dowling Singh is trained academically in transpersonal psychology and works as a mentor for deep psychospiritual growth. She tells us that, "Awakening is far more ordinary and more accessible than we think. In fact, the way we think about awakening can be our obstruction to it. Awakening is not a single Technicolor event for most people, but an ongoing, radiant stance—simple, sane, and ever-deepening dance with grace."[39]

It might seem surprising that no one had ever taken the time to hear Dick's story, but it's true. The bigger surprise is that, like most of us, Dick hadn't once in his forty-plus years of life been a part of one container where this work was valued, so understanding how his life had been shaped by grace and circumstances had never been a possibility.

Revisiting the past through the experiences of suffering invited Dick to become more reflective, something he'd previously avoided. Events and situations that had been suppressed and rightly blocked by his constructed self—experiences of shame and rejection— slowly came into the light.

Initially, his sharing was more like a report about a third party, so I asked him to slow down and share his *experience*. This meant he'd need to listen to his heart. To survive the pain (affect), his constructed personality had formed primarily in his head. While staying in our heads can help us detach from pain, doing that cuts off our ability to live and lead from the heart. This was a new beginning for Dick—a place of practice where he could support making the shift he desired. Taking time away to reflect on your journey with suffering from birth through the present and sharing this with each other is Step Six.

Robert Sardello tells us:

A practice differs considerably from an exercise or a technique. A practice tends to develop new capacities by developing dimensions of attention that go beyond usual *forms* of consciousness. An exercise such as group work may, under certain conditions, produce a momentary experience of a new dimension, but there will not be enough inner strength of will to continue to experience that dimension. And techniques tend to manipulate, often attempting to make something happen rather than helping others to discover what lies within their own abilities.[40]

For several months, Dick's management team practiced with each other. They reported the experience as liberating, and now their connection with Dick was being transformed. Over the years, I've noticed in every group I've been privileged to work with that when vulnerability is present through practice, a powerful field of presence seems to fill the space. This group seemed absorbed by it. They were relating to each other through eyes of awe and wonder, and they were experiencing capacity that they had not known was within them.

Benner tells us that each of us is present to each other in different ways, but the most common is "preoccupied presence." He goes on to say: "When I say that preoccupation clouds presence, I mean that preoccupation robs our being of the singularity and alignment that otherwise give it luminosity."[41]

Up to this point, the management team had only experienced Dick through his preoccupied persona. Dick's fixation was safety and security, but as he ventured beyond, a depth came to the surface.

Allow Belonging to Open Awareness

At the launch of this work with Dick and the management team, we discussed how our work together would take place through the lens of The Johari Window[42]—a model designed to help people in groups understand themselves and each other. The model encourages participants to share as much about themselves as they are willing. The Enneagram, a system of self-inquiry, is unsurpassed because it brings our invisible patterns into self-awareness and, through the Johari Window, into group awareness.

Dick discovered through the Enneagram that his patterns of thinking, feeling, and acting were associated with Type 7. Sevens perpetually scan the horizon looking for distractions and opportunities to stay as far away from their inner aches as possible. They experienced childhood wounds in relationship to the nurturing energy of their caregiver: they feel frustrated because they weren't nurtured enough, always feeling the need for more.[43] Sevens live primarily in their heads, anticipating pain or pleasure and acting accordingly.

Helping others notice is critical, but before you earn this right, you first must demonstrate humility by owning your own patterns and allowing others to help you.

When managers are unable to stay present to the necessary tension of management team conversations and all the currents of affect, one of two things will happen. They will pull the entire team off course, which seems to be the norm, or, if solid ground has been cultivated, others on the team will notice and playfully help them shift back. This is part of "the work" that management teams must take on if they hope to become sustainable. Dick's management team was discovering this capacity, and they were helping Dick shift by holding a safe space of discovery. Step Seven is to discover your own Enneagram type, share it with your team, and create a conversation about each other's type.

Helping others notice is critical, but before you earn this right, you first must demonstrate humility by owning your own patterns and allowing others to help you. Establishing inner work as a group commitment is critical, and this must first take place with the CEO. This is how a CEO can establish deep credibility—the kind that transcends the need to be the smartest or least imperfect person in the room. If the CEO doesn't nurture this, posturing is a sure bet, and this is how the number of disengaged employees grows. The Enneagram is an excellent tool designed specifically to help us open the door to humility.

As you work with each of the conversations, you will notice the sidetracking patterns in yourself and others.

My Enneagram teacher, Dr. Carole Whitaker, describes the Enneagram as a model of consciousness that includes personality and inner experience—spirituality. Tens of thousands of observations over many decades have shown that there are nine styles. When used properly, the structure of our own personality comes into our view. In other words, we are no longer blind to what others have been noticing for years. With the appropriate support and practices, our structure becomes permeable, allowing essence or *True Self* to emanate. Attention holds the structure of personality in place, and attention uses our life force to sustain the structure.[44]

Letting go of identification with our reactions—generated through affect as our brain predicts an unpleasant future experience—relaxes attention, and the constricted energy that holds patterns in place softens. This is what the management team was helping Dick begin to do. Even though he was experiencing anxiety, he knew they cared about him.

In his groundbreaking book *What Really Matters*, Tony Schwartz shares that in his individual work with Helen Palmer and Hameed Ali, pioneering Enneagram scholars, he noticed that, "each views the personality or ego, not just as an obstacle to essence—a false self—but also as the central vehicle through which to uncover one's true nature."[45] He goes on to tell us that Ali shared, "We could do meditations, certain exercises and everyone could feel wonderful things. However, these will not last unless a person confronts his deficiencies, his holes and goes through them."[46]

Dick's management team experience introduced a unique container with contemplative practices that supported belonging and connecting to self and others, and from this experience, "inner fluency" started to show up. When leaders start to embrace and move through these patterns, change happens. This always translates into fresh behavior as members start to reframe their daily interactions within their company as opportunities to practice. Reframing your company as a place of practice is liberating.

Like everything else in life, your company is simply a strategy for transformation in the service of helping you become who you were meant to be. Choosing to view it this way is empowering.

Because each Enneagram type articulates the fixation and passion that make us captive to our narrow patterns of thinking, feeling, and acting, the model can become an exceptional tool. When it is used as a system of personal inquiry, it can transform your daily interactions within your company into learning opportunities, and this is one way we can create value for each other. Versions of the Enneagram have been around for thousands of years in many cultures. Today, there are hundreds of books, so I won't go into detail about each type, but one particular book, *The Sacred Enneagram*, does a thorough job of explaining the model.

The management teams I work with and the members of my Vistage CEO and Key groups all use the Enneagram to better understand and shift their patterns. If you use this in isolation, though, it provides very little lasting value.

The life-inquiry experiences I have described and the practice of noticing our reactive patterns and structures of personality are what I call "inquiry" practices because we are intentionally delving into our inner patterns. We do inner work to get to know ourselves in the presence of others.

Mindfulness training is an additional tool to add to your inquiry practices. Google, hundreds of schools, CEOs, and management teams are enrolling in mindfulness training because it has the capacity to regather our normally fragmented attention. Mindfulness training can be especially helpful when used with the Enneagram model. Once leaders wake up to their patterns of thinking, feeling, and acting and are mindful of the *currents* of tension, frustration, judgment, disappointment, separation, and boredom, their awareness grows rapidly. This is what we call "noticing." Noticing sponsors awareness by bringing these aspects of ourselves into our consciousness.

For the management team, each of the Outward-Moving Conversations around Growth, Value Creation, Execution, Leader Effectiveness, and Management Team Coherence are practice frameworks where "noticing" can be encouraged. By doing this as practice, a playful tone can emerge.

In my own experience and that of many others, certain kinds of meditation, in combination with the Enneagram, seem to soften the structures of personality, accelerating our freedom. With this, we begin to gain access to a much deeper part of ourselves—the part that is open to limitless possibility and, ultimately, limitless value creation.

The practices that we have been discussing are contemplative. As we practice, the noise that goes on in our heads quiets, and with this, inner silence expands. This is the fertile delta where all possibility exists.

Initially when we turn inward, we encounter strong headwind of distractions swirling about within us, and then we notice how much we have identified with these. Yet these thoughts and distractions are simply like the weather that moves around the mountain or the water that flows through the riverbed. As our practice takes root, we understand that these thoughts and feelings come and go. They are not us, they just flow through us.

As we do the work and our practice progresses by entering the inner movement of release and letting go through meditation, we ultimately find ourselves in a light-filled awareness where complexity and frenzy give way to the deep inner peace of solid ground.

During our time of meditation, practitioners are encouraged to release thoughts as they form, over and over, as many times as necessary. With this, we sensitize ourselves to the experiencing of a "felt sense" of letting go. This experience of "letting go" begins to create receptivity. Further, as practitioners learn to hold the intention of "dropping down into" the core of their being, they experience a "felt sense" of stability. This is often their initial experience of becoming consciously aware of *presence*. This is the place where solid ground is present. Step Eight is forming your meditation practice. The CEOs I've worked with have found a four minute youtube video by Loch Kelley very helpful.[47]

Be Present with Reality and Help Others Be There too

Every time we talk to each other, we can practice. By this, I mean noticing what goes on within and between us. As we do this work with the intention of letting go of patterns of thinking, feeling, and acting, and as we connect with the truth about ourselves, our awareness of others opens, and our connection is strengthened.

If we continue to remain unconscious to our patterns of thinking, feeling, and acting, we have no solid ground for others to connect to, and we unconsciously remain cut off from truth. Your group can help you access this.

Once again, John O'Donohue provides an elegant way for us to hold this.

> This discernment is often easier for your friend than it would be for you. Real friends will never come with a battering ram to demolish the prison in which they see you. They know it would be too soon, you are not ready to leave. They also know that until you see for yourself how and where you are caught, you cannot be free. If they destroy the prison cell, you will inevitably build a new one from the old material. True friendship attunes itself in care to the rhythm of your soul. In conversation and affection your friend will only attempt something very modest, namely, to remove one pebble from the wall. When that pebble of light shines in your darkness, it arouses your longing to become free. This dot of light empowers you, and then, brick by brick, you will remove the walls you have placed between the light and yourself. True friendship trusts the soul to find the light, to loosen one pebble in the wall and open the way to freedom. Massive inner structures begin to loosen and break when the pencil thin beam of recognition hits us.[48]

Reality is not static, and it cannot be defined in a fixed way. Because it has more angles than we can possibly see, reality must be discerned. Discernment is more important than technical skills because discernment is based on the faith that something we haven't seen or experienced before will emerge. The impasses that keep us in the doom loop are mostly within and between us, so we must discern their nature. Discernment is not figuring something out. It is far greater than knowledge: it depends on the body, heart, and mind together, living in relationship with others.

How we hear each other depends on where and what we stand upon. Awareness teaches us to see and know who we are. Anne Hillman, a fellow pilgrim on this human journey, describes this journey into *awareness*:

> We notice first what goes on in our minds, then, drop our attention deeper inside and listen to our hearts and our bodies. Gradually we become more objective about ourselves. As we peel away the layers, we have to get more honest. And the more honest we are, the easier it is to hear the whispered song of the soul. The light is dim in the interior world. It's like sitting "at dusk" and waiting for our eyes to adjust to the dark.[49]

I took up the clarinet because my father thought it was important. As an accomplished musician, he understood something I couldn't appreciate at the time, but now do. While I had no desire to play, he sensed that playing would develop a skill within me that was vital, and he was right.

Anyone who has played an instrument for many years comes to understand that developing a capacity to listen is vital. Listening carefully to discern, in your body, the rhythm and soul of your playing is unifying. It brings all of you into a felt sense of what is good, right, true, just, and beautiful. When listening becomes an embodied experience it leads us wisely, and a fresh path forward always emerges. I know now that this applies in business too.

Practice requires us to exercise our capacities. Through the structures of Outward and Inward Conversations, your company can become a place of practice. As you practice doing the work, the way you listen and feel becomes unified. You form solid ground within, and you become solid ground; and others begin to discover the amazing capacity that is already within them.

The way of wholeness is a path your management team can enter together, and through this, you can achieve long term growth, sustainability and flourish as a leader.

About the Author

Jim Moats is the CEO of Jim Moats & Associates where his work emphasizes achieving long-term growth and sustainability for privately owned companies and the owners, executives, employees, and communities that empower them.

By Using nine specific management team conversations to understand the *unresolved* issues that make growth and sustainability challenging and by bringing into awareness the patterns of thinking, feeling, and acting that have invisibly formed within company leadership, value creation can become limitless.

Jim also serves as a Master Chair through Vistage International, the largest CEO membership organization in the world. He has chaired a CEO and Key Executive group for the past twenty years and has been awarded the Chair excellence award eleven years in a row. He completed his undergraduate education at the University of Nebraska Omaha and was trained as an Intelligence analyst/order of battle specialist in the US Army, serving in Vietnam and Europe.

He has served as the CEO of a software company and as the CEO of an international not-for-profit, and has served in leadership roles in three Fortune 500 companies.

Jim lives in Seattle, Washington with his wife Becky.

ENDNOTES

[1] A 360° review allows self, boss, peers, and subordinates to anonymously evaluate the person receiving the review.

[2] "Wikipedia: John Main," Wikimedia Foundation, last modified February 15, 2019, 01:14, https://en.wikipedia.org/wiki/John_Main

[3] Gallup, State of the American Workforce Report, https://www.gallup.com/workplace/238085/state-american-work-place-report-2017.aspx, last accessed 5/19/2019

[4] Chopra, Deepak, The Healing Self (New York: Harmony Books, 2018), 21.

[5] "Lao Tzu, Tao Te Ching, Poetry in Translation, [Kindle] 2015.

[6] Dan Siegel, MD, *Mind*, WW Norton Company, New York London, 2017, p. 232-233.

[7] Martin Laird, A Sunlit Absence, Silence, Awareness, and Contemplation (New York: Oxford University Press, 2011), 85.

[8] Mark Nepo, The Exquisite Risk: Daring to Live an Authentic Life (New York: Three Rivers Press, 2005), 78.

[9] Kristin Neff, *Self Compassion* Harper Collins: Australia, Kindle.

[10] United States Census Bureau, https://www.census.gov/data/tables/2016/econ/susb/2016-susb-employment.html, accessed May 12, 2019.

[11] E.F Schumacher, Small is Beautiful: Economics as If People Mattered (Vancouver: Hartley and Marks, 1973), 75.

[12] David Brooks, "Students Learn from People They Love," *New York Times*, January 17, 2019.

[13] Robert Sardello, Silence: The Mystery of Wholeness (Benson, NC: Goldstone, Benson, 2006), 13.

[14] "A Conversation in Silence," Harmony Productions, https://harmonyxxx.wordpress.com/tag/kabir/, accessed May 12, 2019.

[15] David Brooks, ibid.

[16] https://www.researchgate.net/publication/227989777_Psycho-sociological_problems_of_a_minority_group

[17] Daniel J. Siegel, MD, Mind: A Journey to The Heart of Being Human (New York: W.W. Norton & Company, 2017), 153.

[18] Siegel, MD, Mind, 163.

[19] Siegel, ibid, p. 237.

[20] James R. Doty, MD, Into The Magic Shop: A Neurosurgeon's Quest to Discover the Mysteries of the Brain and the Secrets of the Heart (New York: Avery, 2016), 230.

[21] Rollin McCraty, PhD, "The Energetic Heart: Bioelectromagnetic Communication Within and Between People," Clinical Applications of Bioelectromagnetic Medicine (2004): 541-562. https://www.heartmath.org/research/research-library/energetics/energetic-heart-bioelectromagnetic-communication-within-and-between-people/

[22] Richard Moss, MD, The Mandala of Being: Discovering the Power of Awareness (Novato, CA: New World Library, 2007), 63.

[23] Judy Brown, "Trough," in Leading from Within: Poetry That Sustains the Courage to Lead, ed. Sam M. Intrator and Megan Scribner (Plano, TX: Jossey-Bass), 61.

[24] David Benner, PhD. Presence and Encounter: The Sacramental Possibilities of Everyday Life (Grand Rapids, MI: Brazos Press, 2014), 53-56.

[25] Siegel, MD, Mind, 50.

[26] Siegel, MD, Mind, 135-136

[27] https://www.drdansiegel.com/resources/wheel_of_awareness; accessed May 17, 2019

[28] David Whyte, Consolations: The Solace, Nourishment and Underlying Meaning of Everyday Words (Langley, WA: Many Rivers Press, 2016), 233.

[29] "The Enneagram," The Narrative Enneagram, https://www.enneagram-worldwide.com/the-enneagram/, accessed May, 13, 2019.

[30] John O'Donohue, Anam Cara: A Book of Celtic Wisdom (New York: HarperCollins, 1997), 127.

[31] Lisa Feldman Barrett, How Emotions Are Made: The Secret Life of the Brain (New York: Houghton Mifflin Harcourt, 2017), 70.

[32] Barrett, How Emotions Are Made, 71-72.

[33] Jonathan Posner, James A. Russell, and Bradley S. Peterson, "The circumplex model of affect," Dev Psychopathology 17, no. 3 (May 2008). https://www.ncbi.nlm.nih.gov/pmc/articles/PMC2367156/.

[34] Lisa Feldman Barrett, How Emotions Are Made; The Secret Life of the Brain, (New York, Houghton Mifflin Harcourt publishing, 2017) p 179

[35] Ibid, p 124.

[36] Daniel Goleman and Richard J. Davidson, Altered Traits: Science Reveals How Meditation Changes Your Mind, Brain, and Body (New York: Penguin Random House, 2017), 290.

[37] John O'Donohue, Eternal Echoes: Exploring Our Yearning to Belong (New York: Cliff Street Books/HarperCollins, 1999), xxv.

[38] Barrett, How Emotions Are Made, 170-171.

[39] Kathleen Dowling Singh, The Grace in Living: Recognize It, Trust It, Abide in It (Somerville, MA: Wisdom Publications, 2016), loc. 63 of 3849, [Kindle].

[40] Sardello, ibid, p. 4.

[41] Benner, Presence and Encounter 56.

[42] "Wikipedia: Johari window," Wikimedia Foundation, last modified April 2, 2019, 23:19, https://en.wikipedia.org/wiki/Johari_window.

[43] Christopher L. Heuertz, The Sacred Enneagram: Finding Your Unique Path to Spiritual Growth (Grand Rapids, MI: Zondervan, 2017), 131.

[44] Dr. Carole Whitaker, conversation with author, September 25, 2017.

[45] Tony Schwartz, What Really Matters: Searching for Wisdom in America (New York: Bantam Books, 1995), 375.

[46] Schwartz, What Really Matters, 419.

[47] https://www.youtube.com/watch?v=fkP1-lin590

[48] O'Donohue, Eternal Echoes, 129.

[49] Anne Hillman, Awakening the Energies of Love (Wilton Manors, FL: Bramble Books, 2016), 117.